Praise for *Blue Movie: Scenes from the Life of a Sexual Outlaw*

Ferris's "just-the-facts" prose reads as both blunt confessional and film notes for a grim thriller. I found myself rooting for him again and again, knowing my hope would be dashed with another scary night. *Blue Movie* is harrowing, heartbreaking, unsparing, and will tell others like us they are not alone.

Alexander Cheves, Author of *My Love Is a Beast: Confessions* and columnist for *Out Magazine*

This book is a rare one. In fact, it is raw, in every way. Unapologetically, viscerally, transparently. Raw sex. Raw addiction. Raw recovery. Raw success. If you want to peek inside the mind of a sexual outlaw with the self-awareness and courage to tell himself and you the full, unvarnished truth, this book will not disappoint. It is truly riveting.

Race Bannon, Author and community leader

Demon twinks, cum buckets, and kidnappings are just a few reasons this haunting tale will go *viral*. In a world where sex defines who we are and how we survive, Ferris reminds us that humans will do desperate, comical, and even dangerous things to find community, especially as queer people. This book proves that pleasure comes with pain, but that's all the more reason to fight for the love we deserve.

Amp Somers, Sex educator and co-host *Watts the Safeword*

As an adult industry professional and someone with a history of crystal meth use, Blue Bailey and I have danced around many of the same flames. My friend Stephan Ferris throws us into the fire in his brutally honest and unapologetic true story of hedonistic self-destruction and great personal triumph.

Sister Roma, Award-winning drag queen activist and entertainer

Blue Movie is a brave journey of authentic vulnerability. Captivating and raw, these scenes from a life story saturated by stigma and self-doubt ultimately tell a tale of agency and self-acceptance. Stephan Ferris calls himself "the original demon twink," but his refreshingly honest storytelling is heroic in a world that continues to shame pleasure-seeking. Ferris is the hero we need in the movement to reclaim sex and pleasure as expressions of radical authenticity, and his story is an inspiration.

Phillip L. Hammack, PhD, Professor of Psychology and Director of the Sexual & Gender Diversity Laboratory, University of California, Santa Cruz

Stephan Ferris has written a courageously candid account of his life as a self-described sexual outlaw, addict finding recovery, and lawyer establishing a professional identity. The disparate strands are laid out in scenes revealing the author's struggle to tie them together — moving through worlds with distinct codes, roles, and norms. The ending is more of a cliffhanger than a definitive resolution. But for anyone yearning to build a coherent picture of oneself using puzzle pieces not normally examined in full view of polite company — in short, for anyone at all — this book will be both a challenge and a comfort.

Morris Ratner, Provost, Academic Dean, and Professor, University of California, Hastings College of Law

Blue
Movie

Blue
Movie Stephan
Ferris

UNBOUND EDITION PRESS

Atlanta

Printed in the United States of America

LIBRARY OF CONGRESS RECORD

Name: Ferris, Stephan, 1987— author.
Title: Blue Movie: Scenes from the Life of a Sexual Outlaw / Stephan Ferris.
Edition: First edition.
Published: Atlanta : Unbound Edition Press, 2022.

LCCN: 2022942537
LCCN Permalink: https://lccn.loc.gov/2022942537
ISBN: 978-0-9913780-7-4 (hardcover)

Printed by Bookmobile, Minneapolis, MN
Distributed by Small Press Distribution

123456789

Unbound Edition Press
1270 Caroline Street, Suite D120
Box 448
Atlanta, GA 30307

For Sean

Subject Matter Warning

The book you are about to read depicts graphic sexual scenes, sexual assault, and suicidal ideation. It also includes drug use in many forms, people struggling with ongoing addiction, and the powerful temptations these activities present. Readers dealing with these or related issues should be warned that the content contained in this book may be strongly triggering. If you are worried that reading this book may trigger dangerous behavior or a relapse, please do not read it. If this applies to you, please return this book for a full refund.

Author's Statement

The experiences depicted in this book are dangerous and potentially deadly. I am lucky to have survived them — myself — at all. Nobody reading this book should interpret what I have shared as any form of instruction or endorsement for self-destructive behavior. Do not do what I did. I share my story so that others might feel less alone and see that there is a path through the darkest passages of life. If you need help, please seek it immediately from qualified medical, mental health, recovery, and social services.

Publisher's Disclaimer

This book comprises a series of recalled scenes from the author's life. It compresses events, experiences, and conversations over time. While it is written in the present tense for effect and to create an active sense of urgency and looming danger, these events are in the past. The views expressed are solely the author's and do not reflect the official policies or positions of Unbound Edition, LLC.

A Note from the Publisher

This book went to press exactly one month after the Supreme Court of the United States overturned *Roe v. Wade*, stripping women of their right to abortion. In doing so, the Court denied women their own bodily integrity — personal autonomy, self-ownership, and self-determination. The depth of this human rights violation reveals a stunning disregard for and dismissal of the sense of agency rightfully held by more than 50 percent of the nation's population. To degrade women wholesale — to wrest away from them the supposedly inviolable control over their own bodies — is as violent and appalling as it is unethical, intrusive, and cruel.

Not all readers of *Blue Movie* will approve of or even tolerate what is shared in these pages. We expect that, as its author already has been reviled and loathed publicly for his controversial work in gay adult entertainment. Likewise, not all readers will celebrate and champion Stephan Ferris for his honesty, transparency, and courage — or his evolution into an unrelenting activist attorney.

Regardless, every reader holds in their hands a loud and clear declaration of bodily integrity. The author has used his body exactly as he chose to for one reason: It is his body to control. He has put his body in ecstatic pleasure and grave danger, both.

He has put his body through extreme tests — of unimaginable terror and unlikely triumph. His right to control his own body as an HIV-positive queer person, no matter the opinions of others, helps protect the bodily integrity — the human rights — of all.

Despite his best efforts at self-destruction, the author has lived to tell his story, to write a book, which is itself the result of bodily choices. All authors, Stephan Ferris now among them, sit for months, make ceaseless notes, pace continuously, type countless drafts, read many revisions, and likely want to curse an unending blue streak at their publishers and editors. Few things are more difficult to do than shape a book, word at the time; few things demand more engagement of the embodied self. Many people claim they want to write a book, but very few can put in the extraordinary focus and work required to do so. Books do not appear magically and fully formed. They come through the bodies — the brains, eyes, ears, mouths, hands — of their authors. As much as any act described in this book, *Blue Movie* itself also stands as an intentional act of bodily integrity by Stephan Ferris. He used his body to make this book, just as he used his body to make the infamous *Viral Loads* video.

Like humans, books too have bodies. The body of the text extends from a spine. The paper has a tooth to it. The pages contain the bits of a brain put upon them. The entire book has a voice. The body of a book results from — gets fleshed out by — the blood, sweat, and tears of the author's body. And readers engage intimately with the body of the book. They run fingers under its lines, put its words on the tips of their tongues, let what is inside it enter them through their eyes or ears or gently sliding fingertips. Reading is as physical as writing.

Bodily integrity — enjoyed, shared — sits at the center of any reading experience. The body of the author chooses to make the body of the book, and the body of the book gets taken in by the body of the reader, by choice. Reading is, indeed, a *ménage à trois*, one in which three bodies make meaning. Consent is required and may be withdrawn at any time. Should readers be disturbed, even disgusted, by parts of Stephan Ferris's book or body, we ask them to pause and realize that in holding *Blue Movie* they are already holding him close, too. They also have the right to choose to close their eyes or to use their hands to close the book and put it — him — away.

It is not a far stretch, then, to understand that the Court's decision to deny the bodily integrity of women poses a threat to the sanctity of the First Amendment and our collective freedom of speech. Speech — whether vocalized or written, broadcast or printed, political or artistic, acceptable or offensive — comes through the body. To control one, to violate one, is to

control and violate the other. The history of pornography —
of blue movies — defines the culture-shaping intersection of
these two fundamental rights.

This is why we have chosen to publish *Blue Movie*. It may
be banned, like abortion, which makes its publication even
more urgent to us. We have chosen to publish it because, like
Justice Ruth Bader Ginsburg, we believe in the power of well-
written dissent.

Patrick Davis
Publisher and Editor in Chief
July 2022

Blue
Movie

The 77 scenes in this book are accompanied
by a soundtrack curated by the author.
Visit Spotify at the QR code below to listen.

Disappear Here.

The syringe fills with blood.

You're a beautiful boy and that's all that matters.

Wonder if he's for sale.

People are afraid to merge. To merge.

Bret Easton Ellis
from *Less Than Zero*

Now this looks like a job for me

So everybody just follow me

'Cause we need a little controversy

'Cause it feels so empty without me.

Eminem
from "Without Me"

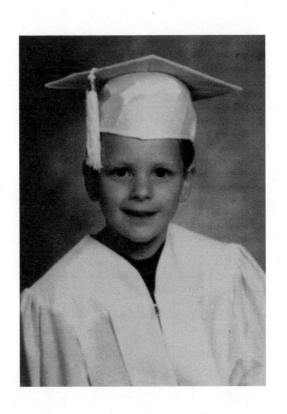

Scenes from
the Life of
a Sexual Outlaw

SCENE 1

I am home for summer vacation. I am knocking out all my appointments, like any young undergrad. Dentist. Doctors. Typical stuff. My grandmother is driving me around Las Vegas. She is one of my four moms: my actual mom, my aunt, my grandma, my stepmom. It is taking a village to raise me.

Two weeks pass. I receive a phone call from a doctor's office. They ask me to come in. This is a tipoff. I am going to be debriefed. I am ready. I am not ready. I go in. My grandma waits in the car. It smells like cigarettes, though it shouldn't. She tells me she has stopped. She has not.

Neither have I: in the past five months, I have had multiple raw sex encounters and multiple IV-drug use events. I do not prepare my own needles. I do not ask if they are clean. I am not a bug chaser. I just want instant gratification. I ignore risk. I fuck risk.

Now, here I am. I do not expect anything. I will not be surprised by anything.

The office is white, cold. It smells like alcohol. I do too. I am hungover. I do not know the doctor. He is some random general practitioner covered by my family's health insurance. He is not gay, and says, flatly: "Your test results came back positive for HIV."

The room freezes. I do not cry. I am not scared. I feel numb. I do not want to talk about my feelings. I do not know what they are.

I ask if there is any chance of a false positive. He says no. He says it is not a death sentence. Our conversation is practical. That's all. I tell him I have to go. It has been less than an hour.

I am 19.

SCENE 2

I am back in my grandma's car. She doesn't know which doctor I have seen. She is driving and singing in her own made-up language. It is a mix of Yiddish and gibberish. Her singing masks my silence. Twenty minutes pass. I process for a minute and stare blankly out of the passenger-side window. I remain calm, perhaps too calm. She notices my energy is off. She asks how the appointment went.

I say, "Not well." She is alarmed and asks more questions. They feel leading, and I am getting upset. I rip off the Band-Aid:

"Grandma, I tested positive for HIV."

She stops the car. "From a girl?!"

"No grandma, I am gay."

In one instant, I come out as gay and HIV-positive. She takes the gay part well, but she is scared by the HIV. She pulls the car over, tears in her eyes. I am her first grandkid, and her favorite.

I spend the rest of the car ride consoling her. I repeat what the doctor told me: "I am going to be okay. This is not a death sentence anymore."

I know I am not going to die from HIV, but I sure as hell am not okay. This doesn't matter. I have to be okay in this moment. I hold my head high and make my grandma feel safe. She is spiraling.

Right now, I am her caretaker. Right now, I am in need of care. This will continue.

I adore my grandma. I adore that she has a big fucking mouth. She is my favorite human being but has no ability to keep a secret. I have to tell everyone right now, or it will leak from her the moment she starts to speak.

I tell my family I am HIV-positive and manage their emotions instead of my own.

I am powerless to change my HIV status, but I have the power to come out to the rest of my family on my own terms.

I get my mom, dad, stepmother, grandmother, aunt, and uncle together in Las Vegas. And I get it done, cleanly: "I am gay. I tested positive for HIV. It is not a death sentence anymore. You do not have to worry about it. I am going to be okay."

They worry about it. They are mostly Jewish, after all. They cry. They are scared, but not of me. They hug me and kiss me. They just need to know what will happen to me. They want me to find love, to be happy. They want me to be okay.

I am again managing their emotions, caring for them in this moment. I do not know how to allow myself to be cared for. I am now an expert on HIV. It falls to me to educate and console my family.

I am going to be okay.

SCENE 3

I am in high school. I am overweight, with thick glasses, braces, and a rollie backpack.

I am not out, yet, and know only one or two guys my age who are gay. But even they want nothing to do with me. No one finds me attractive — guys or girls. I do not find myself attractive. I have low self-esteem. I am the quintessential loser.

I am with a boy from my class, not as boyfriends, just as fellow outcasts. We meet up after school, at his place while his brother's out. I do not know how it happens, but we end up sucking each other off. This is my first sexual encounter.

I now have a crush on this boy.

AOL Instant Messenger

ME: That was hot

Angelus87: yes

ME: I wanna do it again soon

Angelus87: sure

ME: Where did u learn to suck cock like that??

Angelus87: around ;)

ME: Can you teach me?? I really wanna learn how to suck dick good

Angelus87: sure

Since our first encounter, we exchange AOL messages for several weeks. He has so much more experience than I do. I feel like I finally have someone I can relate to, someone who doesn't think I am weird, or ugly, or too queer. I want him to teach me how to do things right — kiss, suck a dick, jerk off another cock. Finally, my pent-up, puberty-fueled sexual energy has found an outlet. My crush feels authentic. It's not a desperate fixation on a girl in class or some obsession with Alyssa Milano on *Charmed*. This person is right here, in the flesh.

For once, this feels real.

ME: I really like u

Angelus87: k

ME: When can we get together again?

ME: Hello?

ME: Are u there?

Everything goes well until it doesn't.

ME: How could u do that?

ME: Why did u share everything we've talked about with ur friends?

Angelus87: because ur a loser. i don't wanna hang wit u anymore

ME: Do u have any idea what uve done?!?

ME: Now everyone knows I'm gay

Angelus87: yup

Though my close friends at school are all fine with it, I cannot come out to my family. Not yet. I am ashamed of my attraction to men.

I feel alone. I am alone.

SCENE 4

I am in college — San Francisco State. My experience in high school taught me a valuable lesson: Fucking within your circle of friends is always a liability.

So, I don't do it.

I find anonymous partners through various hook-up websites that I have joined since coming to college. This is San Francisco, after all. I find websites like this through ads in the gay porn magazines wrapped in plastic at bookstores or featured in gay media like *Queer as Folk* and *Not Another Gay Movie.*

Right now, I am in the backseat of a car that belongs to a random guy who I met on the website Manhunt. Nothing about him stands out for me to remember him well, except that he has a girlfriend and takes care of her child.

Oh, and his dick smells incredible ... sweaty, ripe, and musky. And it is thick.

He uses a condom, and it hurts like hell when he thrusts his dick in me. We meet up a few times in the backseat of his car, and I always leave with a sore ass and wet baby face smelling like his dirty cock.

Bottoming is so unpleasant. I tolerate it because I am so desperate to experience sex and intimacy. I am desperate to feel wanted and, I guess, cared for. I start to meet up with bottoms that I find online.

I am a total top, bro.

This is my way of protecting my ass and my young sense of masculinity. The way I figure it, if I am the top, then I am the masculine one. This makes my sexual encounters more palatable to my struggling ego. I only fuck strangers, using websites to find my conquests, using them only for sex and validation. I am gay, but I am not a bottom. I am still a man.

I am not a faggot.

SCENE 5

I am a frat boy. I have joined the Pi Kappa Phi fraternity to feel more masculine. It has only made me an alcoholic. Other guys smoke some weed or do a bump of coke.

I just drink, constantly.

✛ ✛ ✛

I am smoking meth. I am 18 — still a freshman — and have not even smoked cannabis or snorted coke. I am with a random Daddy that I have met on Manhunt. We are in his living room, chilling on the couch; the drugs are on the glass coffee table. The house is a mess, stacks of paper and clutter strewn about. But I grew up with a messy father and it doesn't stand out.

The Daddy finds out that I don't find bottoming pleasurable — that it hurts — and he proceeds to place the pipe in front of my face, saying: "It will help you to love bottoming." He teaches me how to smoke from the pipe and I pick it up quickly.

The sex is great. Bottoming is great.

I leave his house in the late evening. I want more. I ask him when we can play again, but he hesitates. He wants to space out our interactions, so I don't do too much and get hooked.

I do not want to play without it ever again.

SCENE 6

I am asked to join a circle jerk by some guy I met online. It will be taped for a studio called Defiant Boyz. There is no audition. I use the name Danny Ryder.

I am in an apartment in San Francisco's Castro District. I jerk off with a bunch of other guys. The one who recruited me never shows.

Being taped having sex is taboo and that turns me on. Somebody wants to film me doing it, and that is indescribably validating for me. I hate my body. I still feel like an overweight kid. When I put on weight, even muscle, I feel fat. I start a gym routine. But what really helps me slim down is partying, playing for days, and not eating.

I am emaciated. I am fat. I need love and care and a sandwich. I hit the pipe.

People want to pay to see me naked. That counts for something. That counts for a lot.

I call myself a model. I am a model. I am condemned. I do not have a future. I am a model. Consume me. Rewind. Consume me again.

None of this matters.

I get A's. I letter in Varsity Quiz. I volunteer. I am a member of the National Honor Society. I am a dork. I am a reject.

USC. *No.*

UCLA. *No.*

Film Schools. *No.*

I do not follow the rules now. The rules do not work.

Fuck it.

"Ready on set."

Let's go.

✦ ✦ ✦

Now, I am Blue Bailey. Now, I am ashamed of my Defiant Boyz days. Now, I am skinnier. Every day, I am skinnier.

I am skinny. Unhealthy skinny. But men like this. Men like little white boys getting railed. The attention emboldens me, and the defects deepen inside.

I am the original demon twink. I am drunk and messy and horny. I cause havoc in every establishment in the Castro. I shatter a glass door, trying to get into a bar after closing. I owe them $600. I am cute and a neighborhood boy, so I am not criminally charged.

I am charged. Charged positive.

I have to go.

SCENE 7

I am in a bar, on my knees. Tonight, I am ready to suck a lot of dick. I have a goal: to get fucked. That's why I suck dick. To get guys hard and then get them inside me.

Paul Morris, the owner of the infamous Treasure Island Media, wants to feature me in a movie as "the best cocksucker in San Francisco." He knows I am a deepthroat expert. He doesn't know I am more turned on by eating a hairy hole. Honestly, I despise the "gag-the-fag" cock-sucking experience that a lot of men seem to like. There is no quicker way to turn me off than to push my head down and make me choke. I am going to puke.

✦ ✦ ✦

I just threw up on a dick. The cameras are still rolling. It is all captured, and I am embarrassed.

Nothing feels sexy now. I am a good bottom, so there is nothing but a light salad in my stomach. The dick hits my throat in just the right spot and — oh, god — here it comes: bile and spit everywhere, with one large piece of undigested lettuce stuck right on the head of the guy's dick.

I clean up. The producers promise me that the disastrous scene will be edited out. That isn't entirely truthful. The scene is cut from the final video, but a clip of it is on the company's blog. I am mortified and ashamed. Every time I see it, I relive the experience. I am going to be made fun of. I reach out to the producers, and they respond:

> There are a couple of other blooper-like clips that are going into the film. The idea is to show that these things happen in real life, and since we strive to be as authentic as possible Paul wanted to show that sex is not always pretty. We particularly like your scene because neither of you took the incident too seriously. It is very fun and shows you guys are pros. I hope you can see it that way ... The fact that you are a little upset about the scene can be used to our advantage if you'll let us talk about it. We can use the controversy to stir up buzz about the film and get people interested.

I do not think I consented to this public humiliation when I signed the release with the studio. Consent changes moment by moment. Still, I decide to ignore the pit in my stomach. I swallow my resentment and keep my mouth shut. I want to be Treasure Island Media's next pass-around power-bottom.

I will not let a little lettuce get in my way. I am not difficult. I am not a diva. I am professional. I am replaceable. I am quiet.

+ + +

I am a bottom. I like being in control. I do not like when control is taken from me. My life is defined by rejection. Now, I curate my image and my sex skills. I do not allow myself to be seen ever — not in an off-putting light, not the real me. I reject reality. I do not choke on a dick and puke up salad. I am in control of when I give up control.

I am told to be louder on set, to play up being verbal. I feel like I must be failing. Can the viewer not tell how much I love dick unless I am verbal? I am not here to perform. I am here to get fucked, for real. I am not a flight attendant announcing what to do: put on a mask, tighten a belt, bend over, prepare to crash. No. I know this trip. My hole can take a pounding. I moan and grunt when it feels right, if it feels right.

I am here for the endurance of the journey, the long haul. I am calm. I let it happen. I put my head deep down into a pillow. There is no noise.

I am flying.

SCENE 8

I am in some guy's dungeon space. It is just us and we wait for some more guys to come over so they can fuck my ass. I am in the sling, just chilling, doing French homework.

Though I continue to meet up with random guys, doing meth before they pound my hole, I am always particular about getting my homework done.

I continue to meet up and play with the Daddy that first introduced me to the wonders of meth. After our first meeting — when he wanted to space out our play dates, so I didn't get hooked — we met up the following weekend to play, to smoke, and to play some more. And the next weekend after that, and ...

Now, as I scribble out some French, rocking back and forth in the sling, I can't wait for the guys to pile in. Though I am not sure if I am more excited about the guys, or the meth.

There are always more guys, more meth, more guys, more meth, and ...

SCENE 9

It is the early morning hours of ...

I have been skipping classes for a couple of weeks, so now I don't know what day it is. At first, I skip just my early morning classes. Now, I have stopped showing up entirely. It is not worth leaving the play parties for two hours to go sweat in class, pretending to be a student.

I am tired of pretending to be everything I am not.

✛ ✛ ✛

I am about to scratch my fucking eyeball out of my head.

I have been up for several days, and I am trying to take my contacts out. I cannot get a grip on the contact in my right eye, and I have been messing with it for the past 20 minutes. I have touched my eyeball so much it is now beet red, swollen.

Wait. There is no contact in my eye.

✛ ✛ ✛

It has been less than a year since I took that pipe from the Daddy for the first time.

I now have a tight band around my bicep. Another random Daddy has a needle in my arm.

Slam.

Cough.

Disappear.

SCENE 10

I don't have a lease or a place to call home in San Francisco, so I go back to Las Vegas. I barely stay awake for the 10-hour drive. I'm spun. My arms are covered in bruises. My body is covered in hives.

I crash hard at home and wake up a full 36 hours later. My family is concerned. I am concerned.

✢ ✢ ✢

I hate it here. I hate being gay here. I hate being positive here. I hate having to rely on my family for money — for car rides. All my activity is monitored. I start resenting tweakers. I no longer have kindness or compassion toward people who use meth — they are gross; they are unworthy of my time and energy. I am superior to meth users.

This strategy is cruel.

I am cruel.

I aggressively condemn meth use to save myself. I am an asshole to people who hit me up online with capital Ts.

I post screenshots of these private messages from guys online. I need to put distance between me and meth.

My behavior is disgusting and reprehensible and effective. Being an asshole to meth users keeps meth users away from me.

I can now go out, do bumps of coke, roll, and manage to not pick up the pipe. I can even find guys who use meth and want to get roughed up. I go and beat them and punch their holes. I walk out of their places in better condition than I leave them.

SCENE 11

My exit strategy is not working. I use a lot, and my world is very small. I do not fear dying. I fear being unloved. No boyfriend, no lovers. Always here. Always now. Alone. I am living out a broken life. I am broken. My blood is broken. My mind is broken. I am a toxic mess except to other broken people like me.

I am a toxic dump of methamphetamines, semen, and emotion. A toxic cumdump filled by men and needles. I am a wasteland.

Who needs real love? Slams are injectable love. Who cares if it is artificial? The feeling is real when it is in me.

I live in a small blue room with my sweetly singing Jewish grandmother. I sneak out every night to inject love.

SCENE 12

I am roaming around Hawk's Gym. I am here with a Daddy I party with, and we have been cruising all night. I taste the saltiness of G in my mouth and take a big sip of Gatorade to wash it down. I leave the bottle in my room and get to work in the hallways.

The G kicks in, and I start swaying to the beat of the industrial bathhouse music. I see my Daddy in a doorway chatting up a big hairy bear. We are not in a relationship, but he looks after me. He sees me and motions for me to come over.

The bear is not particularly attractive, but he has a big dick, and he smells great. Daddy tells me to start sucking. The bear's dick smells great too. Tastes even better. Daddy closes the door to the room. He dims the light.

The G kicks hard. I go cross-eyed while sucking. I am not doing a great a job. Daddy tells me to get up on the bed and show off my hole. I try to bend over on all fours but fall flat on my stomach.

The bear has a raging boner. I am fading in and out. I tell Daddy I want to go back to my room. He places his hand over my mouth and shoves a bottle of poppers under my nose. I cannot breathe through my mouth. I am forced to inhale the poppers.

The bear climbs on me. In a singular motion, he spits on his dick and is inside me. The full force of his body weighs me down. He starts to thrust. I struggle to move. I am pinned down.

I blackout.

SCENE 13

Being HIV-positive leads to a lot of rejection. Even with condoms, nobody wants to fuck me. That's why I stick with my pride of POZ brothers. When I sleep with negative guys, they freak out. They get violent.

It's four a.m. and I need a ride home. My dad picks me up from Caesar's Palace. I am wearing a leather harness, a shredded shirt, and new bruises. I am scared and embarrassed. My dad wants to go find the guy who beat me up.

Disappear.

✧ ✧ ✧

"You're gross."

"You're disgusting."

"You're spreading AIDS."

"You're going to go to hell."

I hear it all. I hear it all, all the time. I hear it from gay men, my own community. I do what they do. I just dare to do it on camera, to do it honestly. I have natural sex, and a lot of it. They call it "bareback" and put their stigma on my body.

I get drunk, high, and horny.

I start working for my dad's moving company. I hate the physical labor. I hate the monotony, even if I enjoy sniffing men's underwear when I pack up their laundry baskets.

I save money and move back to San Francisco.

Las Vegas is where I call home. Las Vegas is not my home.

✧ ✧ ✧

Men in San Francisco are nicer. More people have HIV. More people have died. More people have grieved. More people have compassion.

I get control of myself and reject rejection. I do not date HIV-negative guys. I find my POZ brothers and daddies. They teach me what I need to know, how to care for myself, how to live. They prove to me I will be okay. They save me from myself.

They are my home, these men of San Francisco.

SCENE 14

HIV is not just a virus. It is an identity, a community, a bareback brotherhood: #BBBH, #POZ. Every person with this identity, every member of this community, is a hero. They hold me, and together we find our power.

I reject stigma.

I reject fear.

I reject control.

I reject rejection.

I am not a reject when I reject. HIV makes me triumphant. HIV makes me live. HIV fuels me. HIV has to work hard to get me. I am stronger than it.

I am going to be okay.

SCENE 15

Him: Free tonight?

ME: Yes. At dinner right now. Available after.

Him: Text me when you're done.

ME: What're ur interests? Location?

Him: Top. Green.

ME: Alright. I can probably be there by 10:30. That work?

Him: Should work.

✢ ✢ ✢

Him: Dude! Are you HIV+?

ME: I am undetectable

Him: What the fuck does that mean

Him: !

Him: ?

ME: Means there's zero risk of transmission

Him: So I just barebacked a POZ guy?

ME: Correct

Him: Fuck me. Thanks for letting me know. Freaking out!!

ME: U do not need to freak out.

Him: How can't I? Fuck!!!

ME: I told u I was undetectable and that u did not have

to wear a condom. U decided to take it off. My viral load is suppressed so much that it wouldn't show up in a blood draw ... so u topping me is very unlikely of transmitting the virus.

Him: I am beyond freaking out. NO u just told me to take it off.

ME: I said I am undetectable and u can take it off if ur having issues.

Him: Fuck me! No you did not. I'm just now looking you up online and FUCKING freaking out!!

ME: I am not going to argue with u. I understand ur concern but ur mind can be at ease by checking out info online. U topping a person on meds is very low risk

Him: Very what?

ME: Very low risk. POZ people who take their meds reduce the risk of transmission by 96%

Him: What do I even do now? Dude, I am not judging. But I am kinda freaking out.

ME: Well it feels very judging and pointed at me. If u weren't aware of my status or did not hear what I said then it is not my fault u took it off. Check out PEP program.

Him: Sorry if feels judging. I just did not get it. Nor did I hear you say anything about it. I do not judge you at all. But I am kinda freaked out. What do you recommend I do

now to put my mind at ease? What's PEP? Pls just give me a call back.

Him: Really sorry I offended you in any way. I really appreciate the advice and I had a blast with you tonight. You seem like a real solid guy. I just freaked out and thanks for putting my mind to ease.

ME: Was in bed sick most of the day yesterday. I have to work today but I am pretty open tomorrow.

✥ ✥ ✥

Him: Hey man, hope you're feeling better. So I am still a little freaked out about our hook up. (Again ... NOT judging)! But do you have any specific advice for me to put my mind at ease? What would you do if you were me and had anxiety about this? Would be very appreciative for your insight.

Him: Sorry for bugging you. I am super ignorant on the subject and looking for any insight.

ME: Well, I think it is too late for the option you had. If you want to be absolutely certain you should have gotten a prescription for Truvada (PEP). It may or may not be too late.

*Him: Yah I now realize that after doing some research.
Get it that I missed that window. I am more looking for
what / when / where to go now to give me some peace
of mind. Just looking for a little advice. Are you free for a
super quick phone call tonight or tomorrow?*
ME: Sure. Go to Magnet. Great place.
Him: What's that? Sorry I am so ignorant and inexperienced.
ME: Call me tomorrow evening
Him: Ok. Thank you.

✛ ✛ ✛

*Him: This is John's wife! You motherfucker are going to
jail for not telling him your status!*
ME: My status is always disclosed before sex. I'd recommend
ur husband drink less when hooking up.

SCENE 16

I am awkward and cracked out at home. I am awkward and
cracked out on set. I can't get hard. The footage is unusable.
This can never happen again. This is the first and last time.

The camera hates me like this. I call in sick now instead of being taped messy. I turn down work when I'm messy because porn is not my primary income. This is what privilege looks like. Messy, but at home by choice.

Drugs are explicitly prohibited on set. Drugs are always available on set. Alcohol. Weed. Poppers. I sometimes take a shot of whiskey with the crew. If I smoke a joint, I get in my head. I can't perform like that.

So, I wait.

I shoot, and I get super stoned only when the scene is finished.

I am sober. I am not sober.

SCENE 17

Somebody says sex seems painful and unpleasurable to me. They ask if I have been raped because of how I grimace and moan.

I have a hard time relaxing as a bottom, not sure how to find pleasure for myself. I am just a hole for the top. The truth is, I am not submissive. I am a super bottom, and I am both object and subject. I am a dom bottom. I fuck the hell out of men with my asshole. This matters to me. I want more bottoms to feel their own power.

There is no such thing as a "bossy bottom." There is no such thing as a "greedy bottom." There are just tops who need direction, tops who need to be dominated. I love sub tops and service tops. They love dom bottoms. And we love each other. Sometimes, things are just right when they are flipped upside down.

This is my hole. These are my rules. Fuck you.

I get off by sport-fucking multiple guys, taking multiple loads, and bouncing on double penetrations. I will gangbang as many men as possible. I will gangbang the fuck out of them. I will gangbang the cum out of them. They think they are fucking me. They do not know they are just a dick on legs. They are merely penetrating me. I am fucking them.

✤ ✤ ✤

I dream of being Dawson, the unforgettable power-bottom star known for taking lots of loads — 20 loads, 50 loads, and more during a weekend. Dawson is my idol, my hero. I love his unapologetic, fearless approach to using his hole, to taking — possessing — dick. He works for his pleasure alone, embracing the power of his selfish hole. He takes what he needs and wants. He is no secondary accessory to the top. He is not humiliated, emasculated, or degraded. He flips the script on masculinity by celebrating his ability to take dick. He harvests seed. The countless tops are his accessory, in his service.

He is my role model. Now, my butthole will out-dom his. I wear out tops, then line up more who can handle the job. I am no passive cumdump. I actively *take* dick. I actively *take* cum.

Dawson teaches me to be merciless in my dominance over tops. I extract their loads, like a serial killer collecting a trophy. I use my asshole to steal my tops' DNA. A bit of their soul now belongs to me, absorbed into my very being. Dawson shows me who I am: the Alpha Bottom.

✢ ✢ ✢

The T-shirt I am wearing reads "Have You Fucked Dawson Yet?" I rent his videos from Super Star, the rental store in the center of the Castro.

I rack up an absurdly high amount in late fees from not returning *Dawson's 50 Load Weekend* on time. Finally, I decide to pirate the movie and burn the DVD.

I do not have a DVD burner, but my fraternity brother does. He is my big brother, and muscular and sexy as hell. He is also incredibly straight. He is cool with gay guys. I am nervous to ask, but he agrees with no pushback. I put the disk into a blank case, so he doesn't openly have the cover of a pig bottom video in his bedroom.

I get a text: WHAT THE FUCK DID I JUST WATCH?!

His girlfriend is my best friend, and when we hang out it is to watch campy teen dramas on the WB. He thinks my request for a copied DVD is for *Dawson's Creek*. He is wrong.

We laugh. There is no future chance for him to burn another DVD for me. That's OK. I take what he has to give me.

I have my trophy.

SCENE 18

I wake up to the beating pulse of dance music outside my window. I am freezing and covered in sweat. The sun is down. I have slept all day. The party for this year's GAYVN Awards has started. I am at the Blue Moon Resort in Las Vegas.

My throat is scratchy, and I am coughing intensely. I wait in the room while my boyfriend goes to find a thermometer. My fever is above 100 degrees.

I am miserable missing out on the fun — hearing everyone else have fun. I am miserable hearing them fuck in other rooms. I am miserable inside and out. This is killing me.

Overnight, my fever spikes. I am having trouble breathing. I am sweating and am under layers of blankets. My teeth are chattering. I go to the emergency room. I am admitted and an IV gets started. The prick of a needle but no rush through my veins. This is killing me.

They think I have tuberculosis and quarantine me. The test comes back negative, and I hope to leave so I do not miss the entire party. I am stuck in a hospital bed alone while all my friends fuck. I want to see the awards ceremony, if nothing else.

My family visits and drops off a portable DVD player. Two of my porn producers stop by, too.

Bloodwork confirms I have pneumonia. Bloodwork confirms I have an incredibly high viral load. My CD4 count is 198. Technically, I now have AIDS. TKO.

Everybody keeps saying I am going to be okay.

This is killing me.

✛ ✛ ✛

I am in the hospital for a week. I start medication to control the rampages of my HIV. As always, I manage viral loads like a champ.

The new drugs — these meds — give me vivid, disturbing dreams. My baseline is vivid and disturbing. I am vivid and disturbing. All great horror movies get inspiration from nightmares. I do not see Michael Myers or Jason Voorhees or Freddy Krueger. I dream I am using. The meds — these new drugs — cause mood swings, disorienting me and amplifying depression and anxiety. Doctors say they will make me a little crazy. I am a little crazy.

This is killing me.

✛ ✛ ✛

PrEP prevents HIV transmission better than condoms. I test positive just before PrEP becomes available.

The AIDS Healthcare Foundation campaigns heavily against Truvada, the drug used as pre-exposure prophylaxis against the virus. They call it a "party drug." Gay men using PrEP saves lives. Gay men using PrEP makes the AHF irrelevant. Survival of the fittest faggots. AHF fights life-saving advances as its own life-saving advance.

This is killing way more than just me.

SCENE 19

People are starting to notice me. Guys are writing to me. They want to be the next gangbang power-bottom for Treasure Island Media, as if I know how. Becoming a cumdump doesn't just happen. It is hard work. It is a long wait. It takes me more than two years to earn my spot. You have to stand in line with every other desperate hole. You have to want it, not just ask for it. You have to work for it. You have to earn it. No studio is going to invest in your fantasy.

There is nothing organic about lining up a bunch of aggressive pig tops. It takes time and money. Things are more complicated in real life. It is tough being a professional slut.

Paul Morris, the reclusive owner of the studio, still insists I be known as "San Francisco's best cocksucker." He keeps offering me oral scenes. They are not fun. They are not fucking. I do not like them. I do them. I know my place. If I obey, I might get chosen. Who do I have to blow to get fucked around here?

✛ ✛ ✛

It has been nine months of cock sucking and more cock sucking. Finally, the call comes. I am cast as a bottom in a Treasure Island Media movie. Things are lining up. I am riding in the AIDS / LifeCycle from San Francisco to Los Angeles. The shoot is in L.A., so I'll already be there.

How will I bottom after such a long ride?

How will I get double penetrated with a sore ass?

I do not care. This is happening.

This is not happening. I care very much. I get giardia on my way to Los Angeles. I shit everywhere. I shit immediately when I eat or drink anything. I am furious at myself for being sick. I know this isn't my fault. But this is my fault.

I have ruined everything. My boyfriend is doing the shoot now. He replaces me. He steals my scene. He ruins everything.

I have fucked up. I do not get fucked. I get fucked up. Fuck it. Let's fuck it up.

Paul wants me to get the Treasure Island Media logo — a skull and crossbones — tattooed on my body. He wants me to be one of his marked boys. But I am not public about being an HIV-positive performer. I am not the only one.

I do condom porn. I do bareback porn. I jump between the worlds of safe and unsafe. I am safe and unsafe. I am not the only one.

People perceive me how they want to, depending on the scene I am in.

Who am I? You tell me.

✛ ✛ ✛

Mr. Pam is not a man. She is a powerful super-bitch who takes no shit from anybody. I say that lovingly. I owe all my mainstream porn success to her. She treats me right, and her work gets me noticed by all the big studios. Most studios discriminate against me and do not want to feature me in a major way because I do "too much bareback stuff." Audiences love "bareback stuff," but even in porn, reputation matters.

Bareback shoots are fun. There is real chemistry. We want to fuck.

Mainstream shoots are just work. There is little chemistry. And some of the gay-for-pay guys do not want to fuck — or be there at all. We all watch them watch straight porn so they can get hard so you can watch gay porn. It takes hours to film. Hours of standing around and staying hard. This is a circle jerk of watching. Watch out. Nothing in mainstream porn is real.

✛ ✛ ✛

I decline the tattoo.

SCENE 20

I am in the emergency room, again. This is the third time for the same thing. Priapism. My dick has been hard for hours and will not go down. This is not fun. It is dangerous. It causes permanent damage to the interior of the penis. I have been erect for 12 hours. I am in excruciating pain. Each heartbeat feels like my dick will explode.

The first time this happens, I get a shot of epinephrine into my dick and it goes down. Not fun. Not great. But done.

This time, the epinephrine does not work. The only solution is to drain my dick. The doctor has to squeeze my dick, and I nearly pass out. Then, he jabs a needle into it to get the trapped blood out. I am dying. He isn't finished with me yet.

He wrings my dick like a sopping wet towel to get the blood out. I have no context for pain like this. It changes me. This has to be repeated twice in 24 hours because my insistent erection comes back. I'd rather be dead.

This is because of Trimix, or what some people call "liquid Viagra." It is actually a combination of three erectile medications. It is injected directly into the side of the dick.

I did not inject it into myself. A studio assistant did. I told him not to use very much. He did not listen to me. Studios have been sued for dispensing and administering Trimix without any

medical training or prescription. The studio pays for the ER visit.
I stay quiet.

I do not top anymore with my dick. Too dangerous.
Occupational hazard.

SCENE 21

Enough of the run-around. I take my destiny into my own hands. I
email Paul Morris directly. I know what I want.

Greetings,

I have filmed for you several times as an oral boy,
but never really got to show off my bottom skills.
Life with the partner doesn't allow me to take as
many big raw cocks as I'd like, so maybe you can
help me out here. Been working out and certainly
have had my gangbang cherry busted. Attached are
some recent photos from a shoot I did. Look forward
to hearing from you.

Regards,
Blue Bailey

I send my email at 11:41 p.m. Paul responds within 15 minutes.

Hi Blue,

How many loads are you willing to take for me?

PM

This is the birth of *Viral Loads*. I am fucked by 21 men. A Mason jar filled with more than 200 HIV-positive loads is poured up my ass through a tunnel buttplug. What do I care? That's a small price to pay to get what I want.

I have no input into the marketing of the video. I have no idea it appears to viewers that I am HIV-negative. I have no way of knowing the title of the movie until it is released. Some people say it is among the most disturbing and controversial porn ever made. Some people think I am the devil. Some people think I should die for it.

I get paid $1,500. I would have done it for free.

SCENE 22

It is Dore Alley Weekend, and sex pigs from across the nation are in San Francisco. A blast email goes out calling countless anonymous men to participate in a gangbang. I will be their hole.

SCENE 23

I wake up to a text from Mr. Pam. Still not a man. She wishes me luck on my gangbang. She says, "break a leg." I say, "bust a nut." I am nervous. I bottom a lot, but this is a whole new level.

What if it hurts? What if I need too many breaks? What if my hole gives out right in the beginning? What if I my clean out doesn't take? There are a million ways this thing can go wrong. There is no backup bottom. It all hinges on me being able to perform.

I eat light. Protein bars and shakes. Absolutely no salads. *That* is not happening again. I drink coffee. I shit. I douche. I take Imodium. I douche again. I am good to go — I hope. I head out to the shoot and arrive before all of the tops. I fill out my paperwork, drop off my bag, and wait in the lobby. I position myself to watch the elevators, and I see the tops — the strangers, my breeders — arrive and go up to the room.

It is hot outside. My legs stick to the leather seats as I await a text saying it's time to go up. It comes. More will come. There are 21 men waiting for me.

+ + +

The entire scene takes just three hours. The men do their job. I do mine. I am sober the entire time. I know what I am doing. Now, I am full of their seed, and the jar of jizz that has been collected during a week of harvesting others. I ask no details about it. I want the dark magic and impossible mystery of what will be in me.

Someone is hired to be the official felcher of the scene.

My fantasy is now reality. I best the single-scene record for loads, surpassing Dawson. He took all weekend. I took just three hours. I am my new idol. I am on an endorphin high. I am infamous. I have my trophies. I am my own trophy case.

My stomach is exceedingly sick for days.

+ + +

Viral Loads drops just as I start law school.

Some people say, *let's kill all the lawyers*.

SCENE 24

People with HIV get shamed. People on PrEP get shamed. Shame is universal. Choose: Whore or Truvada Whore. One way or another, a pill now defines nearly every homo.

The AIDS Healthcare Foundation spreads fear. They want us to fear each other. "Trust him?" their ads caution. Yes, I do. He is my brother, and we take care of each other. I see AHF as the anti-vaxxers of my community. I do not listen to anti-science fearmongers who aim to pit me against the people I love. I am not a victim of AIDS. I am not a victim of the AIDS Healthcare Foundation.

I am pulled to Magnet, a program of the San Francisco AIDS Foundation. They know me. They meet me where I am, in truth. "Magnet Loves Cumpigs." Me too. Magnet brings positive and negative together, bonded by the force of nature that is cum.

Still, I thank the AHF, a deadly virus of misinformation. I am enraged. I am activated.

I will not let them scare one more young faggot away from PrEP. I speak on every safer sex and industry panel I can. I am notorious. I am infamous. I am loathed. Nothing scares me. I know shame and stigma better than most. I fight the virulent AHF with the truth — personal, factual, legal.

I am fearless. I am living proof. Proof positive. And I am just starting.

Thank you, AHF. Thank you for unleashing me. I am a nightmare of righteous anger. Fuck you, raw. Fuck you, 21 times over. Fuck you, with 200 POZ loads. Fuck you with me. Fuck you and your viral loads of bullshit. Attention whores.

SCENE 25

A bunch of social media posts alert me to something happening. I am not prepared in any way. Treasure Island Media's website shows my face, and it reads:

> *The willing, hungry lad gets gang-fucked by a roomful of studs. Most are POZ, some are neg. Who the fuck cares? Not Blue, that's for fuckin' sure.*

People think *Viral Loads* depicts my seroconversion. My already-positive status is not revealed. Knowing what people think is impossible. They get outraged by seeing men fuck the way everybody wants to. They get outraged by men fucking in ways that have been stigmatized. They get outraged by their own cultural standards being broken. They get outraged by natural fucking. They get outraged by fearless fucking. It is hilarious. It is outrageously hilarious.

For us faggots, HIV is a fact of life. We stand up to it. It happens. It does not steal our sex anymore. It might challenge our bodies, but it does not get our horny minds and hungry holes. Besides, some people fetishize HIV. Get it, and worry evaporates. Get it, and the source stays inside forever, bonded like brothers, like magnets. #BBBH.

With more than 200 HIV-positive loads inside me, *Viral Loads* ends with the assumption that I am now positive. The only seroconversion occurs in the viewers' minds. Fantasy erases reality; reality erases fantasy. The truth positively comes out.

I am going to be okay.

I need my brotherhood. HIV does not threaten my life. Religious crazies and intolerant gay men who send me death threats do. The hate mail is more dangerous and virulent than anything inside my veins.

Viral Loads starts a dialogue, a debate, and a wave of revelations about life with HIV. It is one of the most powerfully political pieces of smut art ever made. I wish I had known what was coming, but that's okay.

I am proud.

SCENE 26

I am hungover. My eyes are dry and red. I get up to take a piss and pop my contacts out. It takes a little more effort than usual. They are stuck to my eyes.

I grab my glasses and I get back in bed. I check my messages. My *Salon* article is live, and my phone is blowing up with tags and comments. It is the first interview I have done since *Viral Loads* released. This is a much larger audience than porn blogs. I am proud of how I handled myself.

In the article, I give my side of the story. I confirm that I am a willing and consenting participant in the video. I detail my testing protocol and disclosure policy. I speak about my assessment of risk and how taking POZ cum as a HIV-positive man really has no substantial negative impact for me. Though I disagree with the sensationalism of it all, I understand it. Porn is fantasy. Porn is entertainment. It is not meant to educate. It is not meant to be a guide. It is meant to be hot. It is meant to get you off. Sex sells. Controversy sells. Treasure Island Media makes a profit off sex and controversy. It is their brand. I know this.

But my brand is sex activism. Controversy has to lead to something more meaningful. Otherwise, it is just a stunt. I am no stunt cunt.

Once the spotlight is on me, I educate on what it is like to be a POZ cumdump. As a performer, I have that power. I have the power to take moments in culture and use my cult following to put my informed view on things. I can enter the conversation with authority. The power to influence is the reason to be part of the controversy.

I use my infamy as the star of this video to spread things — but it is not HIV. I get to talk about serosorting, PrEP, and undetectable viral loads. I get to show others that there is an alternative path to the condom-only definition of safer sex. I get to show that I can thrive sexually as an HIV-positive person. I get the attention of being a perceived threat and the platform to remove threats. Even if I get threatened for doing so.

Most of the messages this morning are in praise of the article. Readers generally agree with the need to clarify the record, to set it straight — pardon the pun.

One message stands out. It is from a friend in San Diego. He is a fellow performer. He is an A-list fuck star, with a perfect body and big dick. It surprises me that I am even on his radar. His message is short and sweet. He tells me to call him. I do.

Him: Hey man, I saw your article!

ME: Great, what did you think?

Him: Why did you say that you are HIV-positive? We just released a bareback scene together. You bred me. People are now going to think that I am HIV-positive.

I go silent and start to panic.

He is frustrated. He explains that he could have easily explained away my status before the article. Now he has no plausible deniability. This article calls attention to my status and the status of everyone I film with. He is in fact positive but relies on the illusion of being perceived as negative. My transparent truth threatens his false image.

He knows all this. He is straightforward about all this.

He is angry and hangs up on me.

SCENE 27

I am a specific sort of guy, for other specific sorts of guys. I am not for everyone. Still, I do get my fair share of fan mail:

ull die young so fuck u im better biatch hahaha

uve grown fat ew

A friend of mine said the government should put you and everyone else with HIV / AIDS on an island and blow it up so we can be rid of this disease. If that happens, we will not have to hear you brag about law school anymore and pretend you have the potential to be the next Johnnie Cochran.

AIDS people like u are disgusting why don't u die fag

Disgusting gay shame on u pig

Crazy but clean and destined to live a long healthy life because I made better sex choices. I am so happy I am not like you.

Also, as soon as I find out your real name, I'll be sure to hand it over to Porn Wikileaks. Good luck getting your "protective order" against that group of people.

What would you do if one of your clients turned out to be someone setting you up as payback because you were nasty to them online?

*I used to hate you because of your bad personality.
But now I feel sorry for you because your goal to make
everyone miserable like you is your way of coping with
the life-altering mistake you made in your life. That's
not our fault and we do not deserve to have our feelings
hurt by you as a result.*

*Ummm you are adorable, but you are getting kind of
fat. Please stop with the Ben and Jerry's already!*

*So, if your law school bs fails completely, are you
going to be like every other ex-porn star and become
a bartender / dj?*

*I have decided to be the better person from now on by
not coming here anymore and making hurtful remarks
about you to make myself feel better. But that doesn't
mean I do not still hate you and your entire existence.*

*Actually, if you're getting specialized subsidized (or
free) housing, free meds, a free (or substantially
subsidized) education and entrance into college based
on your "disability" then it is everyone's concern since
we are paying taxes so cumdump hookers like you get
to get a top notch education*

Sure, I'll go fuck myself since it is safe and doesn't lead to me catching any diseases. I am proud to be healthy and not a whore.

Okay. Better question. Did you cry when your skank behavior resulted in you being another statistic / stereotype / embarrassment to the gay community? What would be your reaction if a fan painted himself blue and committed suicide just to show how much he loved you? I love sending uncomfortable questions.

I feel proud of myself. Not only have I never taken drugs, but I am also a virgin by choice, which means I have no STDs. Isn't it great to be healthy and not worry about addictions because of smarter life decisions?

You should try smiling more when you bottom, it looks like you're in extreme pain when a big dick is ripping your ass open.

How many guys have you infected with your diseased dick and ass?

All you aidsy faggots say that shit over and over. Who
cares? You're all going to die slow painful lonely deaths.

I feel bad for you. HIV+. Prostitution. Promiscuity.
Drugs. Alcohol. Denial above all else ... when are you
going to get honest with yourself and get some help and
get your life together? — A Concerned Family Member

You, sir, are sleazy and shameless. You lack tact,
morality and a sense of common decency. Where can I
find one of you to marry?

SCENE 28

I return to San Francisco State to finish my undergraduate studies.
This time, I have my shit together. I am an overachiever, getting
mostly A's in my courses. I am a good researcher and writer. I earn
two scholarships for essays. I have been off meth for three years.
I have traveled the world. I have made decent money bartending,
and I pay off my credit cards each month.

I write my final media research paper on the social effects of
bareback porn, centering my discussion around my hero, Dawson.

+ + +

It is one year before I start law school. The doubt and self-questioning kick in. After I crashed with meth earlier in college, I do really well. I recover my GPA. But I wonder if that is going to be enough to get me accepted to law school. Given my background in porn and my degree in media, I want to be an entertainment attorney and work with a company like HBO — a place that produces edgy and progressive content that is compelling and impacts culture.

I apply to the entertainment law programs at USC and UCLA. I am rejected from both, again, just like I was with film school.

When the first rejection letter arrives from UCLA, it is hard not to think that every letter is going to be the same. A letter from University of the Pacific, McGeorge School of Law arrives. My hands shake. I open it with anticipation, with dread, my palms and forehead sweaty.

Accepted.

A huge sigh of relief leaves my body. Even if it means living a slower life in Sacramento, this acceptance letter is a symbol of all I have achieved. This letter means that someone else, someone other than my mom and dad, thinks that I am worthy.

I am going to law school.

I am going to be okay.

SCENE 29

I end up at the University of California, Hastings. I get their acceptance letter three days after the letter from McGeorge Law.

Getting into law school is one thing. Trying to make it through law school is an obstacle course of terror.

I write well. But even if I earn decent grades, I worry about passing the bar. The California State Bar Exam is one of the hardest tests in the world to pass and it is expensive to retake. I am going to stumble at some point along the way. Something will get in my way of becoming an attorney.

Even scarier, should I not succeed, I will still be liable for crippling student loan debt. This fear is overwhelming. Along with living in this pressure cooker of anxiety, there is something that I fear everyone will discover. I fear that it will come back to haunt me.

Viral Loads is making headlines. My sexuality makes me stand out for all the wrong reasons.

✦ ✦ ✦

I join the LGBTQIA+ student group. I am an OUTLAW.

I chose to attend UC Hastings because it is in San Francisco, and it is one of the more progressive social justice law schools. By joining OUTLAW, I hope to surround myself with other radical queers. I assume that a queer student group at a progressive law school in one of the most progressive cities in the world will be progressive itself.

It is not. This is unacceptable and I am motivated.

✢ ✢ ✢

I focus all of my time on my studies. Even though my scenes keep getting released, I am not filming anymore. I am starting to seriously question if my experiences in porn will make me unemployable.

Surrounded by whitecollar professors and attorneys, I feel deep shame from being a sex worker and truly fear that my authentic identity will prohibit me from becoming a member of the California Bar or ever finding decent employment.

I silo my sexuality. I bury Blue Bailey, hoping I can turn Stephan Ferris into a polished and well-behaved homosexual.

Here Lies
Blue Bailey
Former Porn Star
May He Rest ... In a Sling

I desperately want to fit in and assimilate into the legal profession. To survive law school. To pay off my loans. It is no surprise that my shame and worry emerge through substance use yet again. I use a variety of substances, but I refrain from meth.

SCENE 30

I am sitting down with my law school mentor and ask him what is appropriate to list on my resume. I have years of volunteer nonprofit experience, and I have published articles about sexual health and HIV. I am proud of all this work. However, my articles and community service are all under my performance name, Blue Bailey. Taking credit for my contributions will out me to any potential employer.

"If you must hide who you are, you are not going to be happy. Being yourself will close some doors, but it will open others."

His advice reframes my perspective, giving me permission to begin reconciling who I was with who I am now.

✦ ✦ ✦

My first step toward self-integration is to run for president of the OUTLAW student group. My mission: To uplift sexual nonconformists through queer anti-assimilation. I want this LGBTQIA+ group to focus on my fellow kinksters and other queerdos. It does not matter that this group is comprised mostly of well-behaved HRC-branded homosexuals. My plan is to fuck things up from the inside.

Assimilation, in the LGBTQIA+ context means centering heteronormativity, and a focused desire to achieve its standards.

> Het•er•o•nor•ma•tiv•i•ty: *the assumption that heterosexuality is the standard for defining normal sexual behavior and that male-female differences and gender roles are the natural and immutable essentials in normal human relations.*
>
> The American Psychological Association

The APA points out that "this assumption is fundamentally embedded in, and legitimizes, social and legal institutions that devalue, marginalize, and discriminate against people who deviate from its normative principle." This is remarkable. Not that long ago, this same organization defined homosexuality as an illness. The APA is in recovery too. We all are, from one thing or another.

From now on, I explicitly and intentionally identify as a Queer FFaggot. I spell FFaggot with double-F's because I love to fist fuck. This abbreviation is common within the kink and fetish communities.

For me, both terms are inherently political identities — both words are terms of endearment. Not everyone agrees. Old-guard leathermen in particular tend to hate being called queer or faggot, and that's valid. These words still inflict trauma despite new intention — despite these words being reclaimed within the community.

Queers are different, uniquely free, fluid. Faggots are powerful, unashamed, divine.

Queers and faggots are gods among insects. We cannot be crushed, exterminated, locked away in jars. We cannot be assimilated, sanitized, defused. We cannot be cured because there is nothing wrong with us. I know who and what I am. I am a proud outlaw.

What is professional? This is my identity crisis.

SCENE 31

I just popped my second pill. I am covered in blood. It is not mine. It's not even real. I am in a warehouse in Brooklyn.

It is the yearly gay ritual called Black Party. The theme this time is "Mineshaft" and there has been an explosion in the mine. I am cast as a dead mineworker. I love dressing up. I love horror movies. I love incorporating blood and horror into my sex play. All I have to do is look cute and play dead.

There are porn stars and drag queens and fierce faggots and stagehands everywhere. My pill kicks in hard. It is my job to be dead. My body is loaded into a wheelbarrow. I roll.

The wheelbarrow with my dead body is rolled through the Black Party crowd for ambiance. Out of the dark sea of people, I hear my buddy jokingly exclaim, "Oh my god, Blue fell out. Blue G'd out!" Covered in fake blood, I burst out laughing. I cannot stop laughing hysterically. It's hard to play dead when you're rolling on Molly. I feel like the girl in the back of the pickup truck in *Texas Chainsaw Massacre*. Drenched in blood and laughing maniacally. Just happy to be whisked away.

✣ ✣ ✣

After my performance, I go in the dark area, where guys are feeling around for big dicks and bigger holes. A few hands touch me, but instantly pull away. I find a boy to make out with. After a few seconds, he whispers into my ear: "I want to fuck you, but you're sticky."

I need to get back to my hotel to shower, or I'll go unfucked all night. I only have one set of clothes, so I wear a towel. The hotel is only three blocks away, and I can walk fast despite the freezing weather. The Molly helps keep me warm.

A car pulls up. Two guys are inside. They ask if I need a ride. I am not going far so I hop in the backseat. I tell them my hotel. The driver says, "No problem."

I pull out my phone to figure out exactly where my hotel is. My location on the map starts moving toward the hotel. And then away. One block away. Two blocks away. The front seat passenger grabs a small pouch from under his legs. He takes out a torch and a glass pipe. Three blocks. Four blocks.

I freak out. We stop and I grab the door handle. It is locked. The car starts rolling again, and I unlock the door manually. I jump out of the moving car.

I make it to the sidewalk. The car drives away. I fumble for my phone and drop the towel. I frantically look on the map for where I need to go.

In the dead of night, I am a naked, bloodied corpse roaming the streets of Brooklyn.

SCENE 32

I fall in love with someone. He uses meth. He tells me how hot the sex is when he uses.

I am reactivated.

I want to have these hot experiences with him. I want to have them for myself.

Because the strategy I use to separate myself from meth and meth users is to incite judgment and ridicule, I actively push users away from me. This strategy fails when the user is my partner, when the user is someone I love. But my judgment prevents me from being caring, compassionate, supportive. I scream at him, call him names, threaten to abandon him.

This is how tough love works. Right?

I don't give him any space to be human. To make mistakes. To learn from them. My cruelty pushes him away, into the arms of substance use — who always has its arms open, its veins ready.

✢ ✢ ✢

The variety of non-meth substances I use quickly escalates back to heavy IV meth use. I binge use. I use for several days. Then I sleep for several days. This process repeats. In the interim, I struggle through my coursework. Somehow, I maintain a 3.1 GPA.

I use with him. I use without him. We fight all the time and accuse each of horrible things. There is no trust between us. There has never been any trust between us. That is what meth-fueled paranoia does.

The relationship ends in violence and contempt.

SCENE 33

I am a West Coast boy and not ready for winter in D.C. It's been a few months since my fiancé left. I am destroyed. I have a hard time feeling happy. I have a hard time feeling anything except for the cold. I need to feel happy. I need to have fun. I need this weekend to be around my chosen family. It is mid-January. I scurry across the street in shorts, a harness, and a hoodie. I dress lightly because I know my journey is less than a block. I am just going across the street from one hotel to another. Once I get inside the next hotel, I'll be warm again. I will not even need a hoodie. I do not want to be responsible for extra clothes during this visit.

A line of men has formed. The line starts at the hotel's entrance and wraps around the building. The men are dressed in leather and rubber. They wear heavy motorcycle and bomber jackets. I make my way to the back of the line, shivering. Droplets of water form on my bare legs as the falling snowflakes melt. I hate lines.

The line moves fast, and within 10 minutes I am inside the Hyatt Regency on Capitol Hill. I am warm again, too warm. I take off my hoodie and place it in the fabric backpack that houses a travel sized bottle of Swiss Navy silicone lube and a large bottle of Blue Boy. This is my go-to brand of poppers.

The lobby of the hotel is teeming with leathermen in varying levels of dress. Some in full formals. Some in harnesses. And some just in jocks. The heating inside the hotel makes it comfortable to wear less. I beeline directly to the elevator, keeping my eyes down. I make sure to avoid direct eye contact with anyone as I swerve through the crowd. I do not have time to stop. I do not have time for pleasantries. I have an objective. I am on a mission.

I get into the elevator. It is crowded and everyone remains quiet. Only a song breaks the silence. It is an old Depeche Mode track, which I love. It is comforting and I listen to the lyrics as they drain over me. *He knows where he is taking me / Taking me where I want to be.*

I get off the elevator and load up Scruff to find the exact room I am going to. It is not too far down the hall. I knock on the door and the boy I have been chatting with answers the door. He is scruffy and short, an adorable pocket gay. I settle into an empty chair in the room and pull out the wad of twenties shoved into my skintight black shorts. He opens a suitcase and starts to pick through a variety of plastic bags. He points to and offers me the glass pipe on a damp white hand towel next to the alarm.

I decline. Meth is not an option for me this weekend. It is my first Mid-Atlantic Leather Weekend. It's my first 30 days. It's my first event being single in a long time, and I have traveled across the country to spend the weekend with my Chicago brothers who are also here. I only want to buy coke. Coke and Molly are part of my harm-reduction plan. I can get fucked up on coke and not get crazy with it. And this weekend, I'll have my brothers around to watch over me. To keep me safe from myself.

I buy an eight-ball. This should be more than enough to last me through the entire holiday weekend. The dealer asks if I want to stay and fuck around. I know from his profile that we are both bottoms, and he is partying. We are really not a match. I do not want to be rude, so I say I'll stay and do a line. There's no harm in getting my dick sucked. I pour out a mound of coke onto the table next to a stack of plastic-wrapped coffee cups, humming the Depeche Mode song that was playing earlier in the elevator.

Promises me I'm safe as houses / As long as I remember who's wearing the trousers.

The coke in the little white baggy is finely chopped, so all I need to do is move it around with a credit card. I roll up one of the spare twenties in my pocket and snort a fat line. I hate lines. In my peripheral vision, I see the dealer pick up the pipe and blow a cloud.

I lift my head up. My nostrils burn. My nose is on fire. I know this burning. I am very familiar with this burning. Coke numbs. It doesn't burn. I tell the dealer this isn't coke. I am upset. I ask what was in the baggy he sold to me. But I already know what it is. He takes another hit off his pipe and walks over.

He wets his pinky, dips it into the mound, and places it into his mouth. With a smirk on his face, he calmly explains: "I must've mixed up the bags. This one isn't coke. It's Tina."

He goes through the motions of apologizing and grabs another baggy out of the suitcase. He offers this to me free of charge for the mistake. My pupils are now fully dilated. I see them in the mirror. My head is spinning. I am anxious, excited. My dick is pulsing on the seam of my jock. I am horny. A bead of sweat drips down my forehead. I wipe the sweat off with the back of my hand, and I shove the baggy in my shorts.

My brain is on autopilot. I go back to the single serving plastic-wrapped coffee cups. I move the mound around again and cut another line. I still hate lines. My nose burns but not as badly as the first time. Now, my forehead and my nose are dipping.

This is happening. I might as well enjoy it. I start to cut a third line but instead ask if I can load up the pipe. I am sniffling because the lines tore through my nostrils.

Smoking is easier on my body. This is one dangerous definition of harm reduction.

He passes the glass bulb. It is already full, but I add a bit more. It is a gesture that shows that I am contributing to this. As I load up the pipe, the dealer asks if I would be bothered if he slams. I say no. He asks if I want one. I say no.

He tells me that he needs to slam in the bathroom. The lighting is better. I ask if I can watch.

We are flying high. I sit on the floor. He sits on the toilet. The floor is cold, but not cold like outside. It is refreshing. I lose track of how many clouds I have blown. My entire body is on fire now and the floor cools me off a bit.

He wraps a belt around his bicep and balances his arm on the toilet paper fixture. He sticks the needle into his arm, pulls the plunger back, and the syringe fills with a red cloud. He slowly pushes the plunger half-way down and stops. He looks at me with the point still in his arm, and calmly says: "Hey, handsome. Would you like the rest of this?"

My dick pulses even harder. I should say no. I do not say no. I have been bred by cum but never by blood. This is harm justification.

I say yes. I stick out my arm.

See the stars, they're shining bright / Everything's alright tonight.

SCENE 34

I like rituals. I like dark rites of passage. I like Point Seven.

This is something I stumble across online. This is something I do. This is something I am scared by and that thrills me. I hear others speak about it with equal wonder and fear. It is a fever dream when I do it. My inner animal goes wild. My private monster breaks free. It is my own horror film, and I love it. The worry, the shaking, the terror. It takes me from mild to wild in sixty seconds. Floor it. Flood me.

I need it. I yearn for it, search for it, seek it out in the darker corners of the Internet. I put myself where it can happen.

I am in fantasy mode — so I can quell this hunger easily, keep this beast at bay, with a video. Never lose control. Never let the monster out. One video shows two guys in a truck. One shows a left- and right-arm dual administration. In another, someone else registers the point with his own blood, then injects his playmate.

Point Seven.

✛ ✛ ✛

"Point" is slang for a syringe or an injection, and "PoinT'" for intravenously injecting methamphetamine, or slamming.

I slam Point Five. I fill the syringe with 0.5 grams of meth. I crush the rock into a fine powder while it is still in the bag. I use the dull end of a pen as my hammer. I dissolve the powder into water.

I have been up for days, and this careful process deteriorates. I deteriorate. I am a mess. I have a tweaker's mess on my hands. Clutter everywhere.

I usually "backload," meaning I fill the syringe with powder to measure my dose. It is not scientific. It is not exact. It is not even hygienic. It does not involve a scale. It is a guess, at best, so I get the high I want. Does the trick, then the trick does me.

The syringe is marked on its side 1 — 10, in measured units. I pull the plunger back. Pop. This is a sound I know well. I hear it walking through dark alleys. I hear it over the music at bathhouses. My ears perk up. My dick pulses. The sound is wedding bells for a tweaker.

I try to find some sort of a clean surface. I use a pen cap as a scoop and transfer meth from the small plastic bag into the smaller tube of the syringe. On day one, I am Ballerina Barbie — graceful, delicate. On days two, three, four, five, six … I am Malibu Barbie — the nightmare.

I scoop a lot and get the crushed meth to the third or fourth lines marked on the point. I flick the chamber to make the crushed rock settle. I add more until I reach line number five.

I continue to add more until I hit line six … line seven. Point Seven. I second-guess myself and pour some of the crushed powder back into the bag. Well, maybe just a little more. Okay, a lot more.

I use insulin syringes. I prefer the short "bee-stinger" needles over the longer points. My veins are easy to find. I can get needles delivered to my apartment. Crisco and Gatorade, too. I am too anxious to go outside. I am too afraid of other faces. Am I seeing them or are they seeing me? Get inside. Stay inside.

I slam with sterile water, with Evian. That's a joke. I slam with tap water. I do not care. I microwave it. It's hygiene theatre, but I think it helps. I worry about bacteria, not meth. It is pure. It is trash. It is pure trash.

Let's get trashed. Trash my ass.

I flick the side of the syringe, needle pointing up. I shake the syringe rapidly to help the crushed rock dissolve. I place it behind my ear to keep it warm.

I like it syrupy, not watery. The syrup doesn't bounce up and down so easily.

It is time — Point Seven. Straight to the brain. A bolt. A bullet. Call me 007. Agent of self-destruction. License to thrill. No time to die. Dance into the fire.

✢ ✢ ✢

I use "admin" as a verb and as a noun. *Can you admin me?* or *Find me an admin!* I know professional admins. One is a nurse; there are no credentials for this. Twenty-five bucks per person, or a fuck. Out the door and about their business. This is slam culture. Welcome.

Trash me.

✢ ✢ ✢

I find and hit my own vein in less than 10 seconds. I refuse to hit others. I am responsible for my slam only. No fuck ups. No overdoses. At least not for them.

I slip the needle in, thread my vein, and pull the plunger back. A plume of red. I am registered. I am an octopus inking through the water. Red is my safe word. Red means stop. Now, red means go. I am ready. Go.

Something is off. It burns. Strike one.

Readjust the needle. Do the delicate work. Pull back again. No ink. I am a dying octopus. Strike two.

New spot. New vein. Thread, ink, push through the cloudy syrup. I raise my arm and try to touch the ceiling. It is just what we do. It is not scientific. It is not exact. It is a slam pig thing.

I cough intensely. It hits. My dark passenger takes over from here.

Off I go, lost to the deep.

SCENE 35

I am a beast. I am set loose. I do what I want. That's the point of slamming. Nothing stops me. Nothing can stop me. I can't stop me.

I am the demon seed.

I am marked.

I am 666.

There are others like me. We find ourselves in alleys, bathhouses, and insanely expensive hotels and glass condominiums above San Francisco. Our rituals require blood and sex, shards and white smoke. We fuck on pentagrams. We fuck on swastikas.

My family is Jewish. I am ruin, awake and horny. Anything that feels bad makes me feel good. I do not care. It pushes my buttons. It pushes your buttons. That makes me cum.

Let's go. Let's fuck things up.

SCENE 36

I feel a satin blindfold drape over my eyes and tied tightly behind my head. The rush begins to wash over my body, part excitement, part fear. My arms, outstretched, expose my veins. I do not know what is happening. Who is injecting me? How much are they giving me? What is it? Is the needle clean?

It is terrifying and makes me hard. I am completely at the mercy of the person holding the needle to my arm. Everything depends on their skill, temperament, and god knows what.

The needle goes in. It hits the vein. The dose is just right. And I no longer need the blindfold because I fall into bliss.

Oblivion.

Disappear.

SCENE 37

I am back in reality. It's dark and I can't see much around me except for the glow of a television in the corner. I hear the upbeat synthpop of some old 80s song playing from another room. I make out some of the lyrics.

Someone grabs my arms. I feel a little prick just under my bicep. My heart starts racing. I anticipate the rush. I anticipate the cough. It misses. It burns. It hurts. It swells. It will leave a mark.

I am marked. In so many ways, I am marked.

The blindfold is better. I like to be watched, not watch. He grabs my arm. He tries again.

SCENE 38

Something is wrong. I know it immediately. I rip off the blindfold and look down at my arm, the needle already withdrawing, producing a drop of crimson that stands in high contrast against my pale skin.

I feel funny. I look over at the empty syringe as the guy places it on a table among others that have been used and will be used again. I do not know what was in it, of course.

My arms and legs begin to shake. At first, just a little. After a few minutes, they are convulsing, and I do not know when or if they will stop.

I am down on the floor. I curl into a fetal position. The other guys in the room do not pay attention to me. They are on the bed, kissing and grabbing at cocks in the shadows. I can't move the entire time they play.

I am trapped in my body now.

SCENE 39

I am in a downward spiral. I inject meth for days on end, crash, and then do it again.

Inject. Crash. Repeat.

I am running my body — my sanity — into the ground though I have never been able to fully commit to drug-driven suicide. But now, something inside threatens to pull me beneath the surface. I feel this pull right now. It is my undertow.

I call a friend. We go to a meeting. It's CMA — Crystal Meth Anonymous. I get a sponsor. I get a therapist. I need a different approach to my drug recovery if I am going to pull out of yet another spiral.

My therapist instructs me to view my relationships with substances the same way I view my relationships with people — to visualize each substance as a person. Cannabis is a person. Alcohol is a person. Meth is a person. And so on, until I have enough substance-people to make a support group circle. My therapist then guides me through each relationship's dynamics.

How does being in a particular relationship with a substance affect me? Does this relationship enhance my life? Does this relationship bring value other than sex? If the value is great sex, does this relationship prevent me from participating in other relationships? Does this relationship isolate me from friends and family? Does this relationship stop me from pursuing my goals? Does my relationship cause me emotional harm? Does my relationship cause me physical harm?

Am I in an abusive relationship?

✦ ✦ ✦

I uncover an entirely new perspective about my relationships with substances. My relationships with cannabis and psychedelics enhance my experiences and don't detract from my goals. However, my relationship with meth is an abusive one. Meth hijacks my time, causes me harm, and shrinks my world. It fucks me up.

Meth is the abusive boyfriend that I keep coming back to because the sex is so good. Meth always promises that this time will be different.

I take active steps to eliminate meth from my life, while still engaging with other substances that are not problematic. My sponsor won't admit this, but this strategy works for a lot of people. I have great success with this for a long time.

✦ ✦ ✦

Now, I practice harm reduction strategies that include abstinence from all mind-altering substances. I still use poppers. I still identify as sober. The attorney in me wants to argue that poppers do not directly stimulate or depress the central nervous system, and thus, poppers do not fall within the scope of psychoactive substances. But ultimately, I choose to use poppers because I like them. They relax my hole, and they are not problematic for me.

I still have to make the conscious decision to not use meth every day. Some days are harder than others. Cannabis, ketamine, and psychedelics are not a problem for me, but to build up my mental fortitude around impulse control, these substances are currently off the table.

Impulse control. A lot of my substance use revolves around impulse control — or the lack of it — so I am finding ways to elongate my internal decision-making process with much of my strategy relying on sheer avoidance of impulse triggers. Mental health professionals — my psychiatrist and psychologist — believe I may have underlying ADHD issues, which affect my impulse control. But my prior substance abuse is a factor that prevents my psychiatrist from prescribing stimulant-based ADHD medication, no matter its medical necessity.

✛ ✛ ✛

I need to be as productive as possible. I am — amazingly — at that stage in my life. Using substances — even "harmless" ones — does not further my goals right now.

My approach is not set in stone. It will evolve over time as needed, as it has before. I write about my substance use to break down the stigma that exists around something that is a shared experience for so many people. I am doing here exactly what I did in *Viral Loads*.

I am not condemning any person's choices. I am not making any sort of moral judgment about using drugs. I write and discuss my experiences to highlight the importance of intentionality.

I am going to be okay.

SCENE 40

I am at the gym. I have a routine again. I begin my workout. I run on the elliptical. I bench press. I squat. I head over to the free weights and pick up a pair of dumbbells. I hold out my arms like I am waiting for a needle. Instead, I curl my arms.

As the weights meet my chest, I feel something in my bicep move. It is the scar tissue from the missed needle. It is hard to the touch and moves underneath the skin each time I curl my arm.

I have been permanently scarred.

This isn't the only one. This isn't the last time.

Reps, bro, reps.

SCENE 41

I play with a guy who is spun out of his mind. I am six-months sober. I am in recovery. Chemsex is still my fetish. The ritual of it, the risk of it, the rush of it. It drives my sexual hunger. I am voracious.

Sober, I seek out chemsex where I can. I seek out guys that party, guys that slam. I use them like I used drugs. They make sex more intense for me. They are my human high. I am a vicarious junkie, a tweaker by proxy.

I am a voyeur of the wasted and wrecked. I watch spun out guys as I punch their holes and it feels like the drugs have seeped into my fists from being inside them.

Endorphins rush my system. No needle. No vein. Just the float. I am going to be okay.

SCENE 42

I work five different part-time jobs to afford to take the bar exam while having a flexible enough schedule to study for it properly. I dream of being successful, not having any money issues. I call this having salad money. I want to be able to go to any restaurant at any time and order a fancy salad, with all the surcharged extra meats.

Until I pass the bar exam, I get deeper and deeper into debt. Trying to succeed is an addiction, too. I cannot stop. It takes all my money.

Do I even have what it takes to be an attorney?

SCENE 43

My plane touches down somewhere in Europe. Did we cross the ocean? Everything is a blur. I squint and think about the past 72 hours.

It is all right there, behind me: success, love, joy to some extent. It isn't mine to keep, to maintain. It is time to live the kind of life I am here for.

I abandon everything, recklessly. I am reckless abandon. My family, my dog, my career, my future. The mirage of it all evaporates. I light the match on my life. Add some kerosene. Let it burn.

I do not deserve success. I do not deserve love. I do not deserve joy.

I walk across the tarmac and contemplate what I am now doing with my life, why I am here — to live the remainder of my life as a sex worker, a committed slam pig, a real-life rush on video, a snuff flick stopping just short of ... Disappear. Maybe. This life holds no promise of long-term success, love, or joy. My life, my choice. Some people just want to watch the world burn.

Let it burn.

✢ ✢ ✢

I wake up. End of fantasy. I am in my bed. This life I do not deserve is still mine. I am sure my nightmare is a premonition.

SCENE 44

I am in England. Leeds, England, specifically. I just took the California State Bar Exam and am waiting for the results. I am ready to blow off some steam. My favorite band, Muse, is performing at a festival. It is my dream to see them live on their home turf. San Francisco and my new life are ready for me once I am home.

Prior to this trip, I contact a guy named Parker, finding his profile on a hook-up website. Parker is not attractive. He is an older bear. I like older, heavier, hairier men. But not him.

I attend the Leeds Festival, and then Leeds Pride.

After, very late at night, I go to Parker's house with another friend. I know that Parker has a dungeon in the basement of his house. It is my understanding there will be a party going on. When we arrive, we find Parker alone. My friend gets uneasy and leaves. Parker and I go into the basement.

A large red flag hangs prominently on the wall of the dungeon, emblazoned with a sharp, black swastika. There are also armbands and other SS attire strewn about.

Like some other Jews I know, I feel empowered by incorporating such taboo imagery into my fetish. In doing so, I tarnish Nazi ideology with my political and sexual identity. Fuck Nazis.

Parker is not Jewish. Parker doesn't play around with Nazi symbols as some form of reclamation or empowerment.

Parker is a Nazi, to the core.

I do not pick up on this. There are literal red flags, and I do not see them. Soon after walking into the dungeon, he restrains me in a sling, binds my wrists with rope and my ankles with leather cuffs. We have sex. The restraint on my left ankle breaks, and he binds it again with rope.

Parker's drugs of choice are "gas" and cocaine. He brings out some thin silver canisters, each approximately six inches long. Parker sprays the contents of the canisters into a bag and then places it over his head. He closes the bag around his neck with either rope or his hands. He does not hold the bag tight enough to suffocate, but it is tight enough for the gas to mix with the air inside the bag. During our play Parker places the bag over my head three, four, five times so that I must inhale it.

I do not normally engage in asphyxiation play. I do not even realize that this is what we are doing. Parker says the gas gives an effect similar to spray poppers. Passing out is an unforeseen and unwanted side effect of the gas.

I pass out at least twice during our session.

I am in the sling and Parker places the bag over my head. He holds it there longer than he does the other times. I have no way of knowing exactly how long. My brain is hazy from the gas. I do not know what happens to me when unconscious. When I come to, Parker is standing between my legs.

"A beautiful pass out" — that's what Parker calls it.

Once I recover, we move to a specially designed chair. It is a brown, wooden, carver-style chair. It looks like it has a toilet seat on it. Before I climb underneath the chair, he once again places the bag over my head. He holds it for significantly longer. The haze comes, but I stay conscious. Parker sits on the chair. It is particularly low, and he has placed an oversized chain collar around my neck that locks my head in place, underneath.

I can barely move. I eat his ass.

I black out again.

+ + +

I wake up. I have no idea how long I have been out. I start eating his ass again, but I get no reaction. Parker's legs are heavy and restraining my arms. I am trapped under this chair because of our respective positions. I eventually manage to wriggle out through his legs and see him slumped over in the chair, passed out.

I pull Parker into a sitting position. The bag over his head is fastened at the mouth, allowing for his bottom lip to protrude from it. I remove both the bag and Parker's leather shirt. Leather can cause people to overheat. I pull Parker off the chair and put him on the floor, on his side. If he vomits, he will not choke on it.

His eyelids flicker. He will come around soon, just as I have done several times already.

I go upstairs, into the kitchen, and come back into the dungeon with a bag of frozen vegetables in my hand. I put the bag on his chest in an attempt to cool him down.

I go back upstairs, and while I wait for Parker to wake up, I check various websites to look for another playmate close by. I make contact with a guy and arrange to meet with him. Parker will wake up soon.

I go back downstairs to check on him. Parker is still passed out.

✛ ✛ ✛

I slap his face but get no response. I do not know how to call for an ambulance in the U.K., so I Google it. On second thought, I do not call. Parker would be embarrassed to have police see him in this situation. I am embarrassed to be in this situation.

This is taking too long. More time passes, and I start to worry. I take a photo of Parker and send it to the other guy I made arrangements with, asking for help. He comes over and tells me: "We need to call for an ambulance."

We begin CPR, but it proves difficult. Parker's jaw is locked tight. We pry it open to force breath into him. The paramedics and police arrive shortly. I give them a brief recap of the night.

I am arrested for murder.

SCENE 45

I am sitting in a police interrogation room. The chair is hard, cold metal. The room is bright, and I fold my arms across my chest to keep the police officers from staring at the track marks and bruises. But nothing can hide how enlarged my pupils are right now. I do not want the police to think I am sketchy as fuck.

I am sketchy as fuck.

Because Parker is a much older guy, the police believe this is a Rent Boy transaction gone very wrong. After arriving in a dungeon to find a dead body, a plastic bag, and a young guy spun out of his mind, I can appreciate their perspective. There is no evidence to show that I was there consensually. There is no evidence that Parker harmed himself.

I sit in this cold room, powerless over the way Parker used his drugs. Powerless over how the police interpret the evidence.

I am powerless.

SCENE 46

I am in solitary confinement.

I do not know how long I was passed out in Parker's house, with his dead body pinning me to the floor. I do not know how long I licked a dead man's asshole. I do not know how long I am in this cell.

I am anxious. I am scared. I am coming down hard off all the drugs.

My door opens, and a police officer escorts me into another interrogation room. There is no officer there. Instead, I see a petite, brunette woman in gray business attire. A large, dark brown leather briefcase is on the table. It is opened, and some papers are beside it.

"Sit," she directs. She announces herself as my public defender and she quickly instructs me on how to survive this process. "Be as transparent as possible with the police." She further counsels that this is not the United States.

"The police here do not care about the drugs" — the drugs are irrelevant to them.

I breathe, just a little bit.

"What the police do care about," she tells me, "is whether you were at Parker's home consensually and whether or not you provided him with any drugs that would have compromised his breathing." I did go there consensually. I did not give him any drugs.

The police find multiple gas canisters throughout his house. They look through my phone messages with Parker. I retrace and relive every step I made since hitting the ground in this country. This includes several meth-fueled hookups prior to Parker.

This evidence tells the police that I was not with Parker as an escort, that I did not provide any drugs to him, and that I was the submissive in the scenario. I had no control or direction over how and when Parker administered his drugs and the bag. Powerless.

With my public defender by my side, the police release me to the care of friends. I wonder if I would be provided this privilege if I were Black or brown.

The police keep my passport and my cell phone as assurance that I will not skip town. The investigation continues.

Now, I can only wait for the coroner's report. It holds all the power. It can release me. It can lock me away forever in an English prison.

Fuck Nazis.

SCENE 47

I am trapped in the U.K. It has been several days since my release, but I have no sense of freedom.

I am told to come to the police station — the coroner's report is ready. I am panicking.

"The coroner has concluded that Parker died from accidental asphyxiation."

All of the blood rushes to my feet, and I release a breath that's been inside my lungs for days. My public defender is beside me. She nods with the slightest hint of a congratulatory smile. I'll take it. My property is returned to me.

I am no longer listed as a *suspect*. Now, I am an *eyewitness* — to a Nazi gas chamber death. I am the luckiest Jew in England.

SCENE 48

This is my exit interview. It is a truthful declaration of the events leading to Parker's death. This is official.

I am asked new questions about the gas Parker used. I can only tell the police what I think it was — an English version of Maximum Impact, an aerosol that, when sprayed on a rag and inhaled, produces an intense effect. I have passed out from Maximum Impact before, several times, so this makes sense in my world. The police inform me I am wrong.

The cannisters contained a derivative of chloroform. Chloroform is toxic to the central nervous system, just like the nerve gasses used in concentration camps. The police let me go.

I escape England, free from the ghost of Hitler.

SCENE 49

I return to San Francisco and meet up with some friends. It turns out that we have Parker in common.

We share our stories, learning that each of us survived him.

"He restrained me, then raped me."

"I went over just expecting to play around that evening in his dungeon but woke up several days later with no memory."

"He knocked me out. My body was covered in cuts and bruises when I came to."

Parker was a predator.

Parker is no longer a predator. He caught himself.

WITNESS STATEMENT

	URN				

Statement of: **Stephan FERRIS**

Age if under 18: *Ov'18*   (if over 18 insert 'over 18')   Occupation:

This statement (consisting of 1 pages each signed by me) is true to the best of my knowledge and belief and I make it knowing that, if it is tendered in evidence, I shall be liable to prosecution if I have wilfully stated anything in it, which I know to be false, or do not believe to be true.

Signature: Date:

Check box if witness evidence is visually recorded ☐ *(supply witness details on last page)*

I am the above named person and I currently reside at the address in the United States given to the Police.

I am a U.S National and reside in California. I travelled to England on ▮▮▮▮▮ predominately to attend the Leeds Festival. I arrived via Heathrow and travelled to the northwest. Prior to travelling to the UK I made contact with the deceased ▮▮▮▮▮ having found his profile on a contacts site. However I expected him to be away at the time of my visit.

I attended the Leeds festival on ▮▮▮▮▮ and returned to ▮▮▮▮▮ or an Friday night staying with a male called ▮▮▮▮▮ who I had been put in contact with via friends in ▮▮▮▮▮. I then attended the ▮▮▮▮▮ with a friend called ▮▮▮▮▮

I first attended ▮▮▮▮▮ on Saturday at some time in the late evening or early morning Sunday. The arrangements were made through one of the websites that I use and I attended the address with a friend ▮▮▮▮▮ made arrangements with ▮▮▮▮▮ for us to meet up at his house. I was aware that he had a Dungeon in his property as there are photographs of it on his profile on the website. ▮▮▮▮▮ booked an Uber taxi to take us to the address and we travelled there together. ▮▮▮▮▮ was alone when they arrived and I thought it a little strange as he had implied that there was a party happening at the location however this did not materialise.

Eventually we both left and went back to ▮▮▮▮▮ However I later made arrangements through one of the websites to go back to ▮▮▮▮▮ house. I arrived at ▮▮▮▮▮ house late Sunday afternoon, and we went into the basement where we had sex on a sling that was erected in the dungeon. I was restrained by being tied to the swing with rope by the wrists and cuffed at the ankle with leather restraints. The restraint around my left ankle broke at some point and so it was then restrained with rope.

▮▮▮▮▮ had told me that his drugs of choice were gas or cocaine. He was in possession of some thin silver canisters approximately 6" long. He would spray this into a bag and put the bag over his head, which he then restrained around his neck with either his hands or some rope. He would not hold the bag tight enough to strangle you, but would hold it tight enough so that you could inhale the gas mixed in with the air in the bag. During our encounter ▮▮▮▮▮ put a bag over my head between 3 – 5 times for me to inhale the gas. The bags that were used were clear, black and possibly a blue plastic one. I do not normally engage in Asphyxiation play nor did I believe we were engaging in asphyxiation play. ▮▮▮▮▮ described the gas to give an effect similar to poppers (amy nitrates). Passing out was an unforeseen and unwanted side effect of inhaling the gas however I did pass out at least twice during this practise. The first time I passed out was on the sling. The bag had been kept on for longer than the other times but I cannot state for how long due to being hazy from drug usage. I do not know what happened whilst I was unconscious but as I came to I saw ▮▮▮ stood between my legs. He described what happened as a "Beautiful Passout." I was allowed to recover before the two of us moved to a specially designed chair. This was a brown wooden carver style chair that looks like it has a toilet seat on it.

I recall being given the bag again containing the gas and inhaling it, before climbing underneath the chair. This time the bag was held over my head for a significantly longer period than the previous times. ▮▮▮▮▮ sat on the chair and I began licking his anus before passing out again at this point for an unknown period of time. When I woke up I carried on however I got no reaction. ▮▮▮▮▮ legs were restraining my arms and I was trapped under the chair to some extent due to the position he was in. I managed to wriggle out from under it, and saw that he had slumped over in the chair passed out. I pulled him into a seated position and could see that he had a clear bag over his head which finished at the mouth so that his bottom lip was protruding out from under it. I pulled the bag off his head and removed his black leather shirt due to the fact that leather can make a person overheat. I pulled him off the chair and lay him on his side on the floor so that if he vomited, he would not drown in his own vomit. I could see that the victims eye lids were flickering and assumed that he had passed out and would wake up in the same manner that I had just experienced now twice. I went upstairs and got some frozen veg which I put on his chest to try and cool him down.

I then left ▮▮▮▮▮ in the basement for around 20 minutes to come around and went back upstairs where I went back on to various websites to look for another partner close by. There was no way to communicate with anyone on my phone in the basement as it cut off my cell reception. I made contact with a male who lived nearby on the website and arranged to meet with him, expecting ▮▮▮▮▮ to have made a recovery. I returned back to the basement and ▮▮▮▮▮ was still passed out. I tried slapping his face but got no response. I Googled how to call an ambulance in the UK on the open laptop. In the basement but didn't call one because I thought he would be embarrassed about where he was found and I honestly thought that he had just passed out. I then took a photograph of ▮▮▮▮▮ and sent it to the other male, asking for his assistance as he had been passed out for some time. The male arrived and told me that we needed to call an ambulance. The two of us commenced CPR at various intervals between us. This was difficult due to the fact that his jaw had locked shut and we had to try and force it open in order to perform rescue breaths.

The paramedics and police arrived sometime later and I gave a brief of what happened which is captured on body worn video. I was ▮▮▮▮▮ interviewed at the Police station where I gave a full and detailed account of the incident and all my interactions with ▮▮▮▮▮

SCENE 50

I am back home. Kind of. I am living in Oakland — close enough. I work as a property manager for the discounted rent on an apartment. I am home alone with my pup, Daenerys, and every light is turned off. The only illumination in the apartment comes from my open laptop.

I refresh a website, repeatedly, incessantly, waiting to find what I am most craving.

STEPHAN F. FERRIS — PASS

A rush of electricity flows through me. Far better than meth, this rush has me bouncing with joy, not fear. I am flying high on endorphins.

I am an attorney.

I pack a bag, head to gym, and fuck my brains out all night.

I am going to be okay.

SCENE 51

I now have a license. I try to get a job doing corporate transactions or something entertainment-related. I want to switch gears and *serve* content creators instead of *being* a content creator, but it's taking forever to happen. Another gangbang offer comes from Mexico, and I decline it, even though I can use the money. I stay in the porn industry, but as an activist.

✢ ✢ ✢

Why does society stigmatize raw fucking? It's weird to me, because there is no such thing as bareback sex. We made it up. Bareback sex is just natural sex. It is not a fetish. It is what every animal does. The AHF wants to prohibit natural sex and sponsors California's Proposition 60 to mandate condom use in porn produced in the state. This is a new level of inhumanity.

Now, with PrEP, bareback sex becomes normal sex again. Stigmas change slowly, though. Straight people have bareback sex — it makes babies. Sex without babies is the birthplace of stigmas. Sex is pleasure — babies are not. Puppies are pleasure. I want puppies, not babies. Puppies and natural sex.

Now there is U=U. *Undetectable* viral loads mean *untransmittable* viral loads. This is my life's theme, I suppose.

I am the real-life story of viral loads.

Because of AHF, I decide to lean harder into activism and education. I do everything I can to help defeat Proposition 60. I am here for this fight and others related to sex workers' rights and freedoms.

The State of California does not care if I make porn. It does not impact my moral character application to the state bar, which looks for crimes. My sex and work are legal. I ease back into some live appearances and start making cameos in my friends' fan-site videos.

Unfortunately, my activism doesn't pay my rent. I start working at a law firm doing buy-sell transactions for car dealerships. I enjoy working for a gay-owned and -operated law firm alongside other leathermen, but it is soul-sucking and a little slimy. I am soul-sucking and a little slimy.

I make good money. I get laid. I get off. I get laid off.

COVID-19 hits. As the newest attorney, I am let go first.

SCENE 52

Here we are again. Back in the pressure cooker. Everything spinning with worry. Everything at risk. How will I survive?

I pass the bar. I lower the bar.

I do not rise to the challenge. I revert to heavy meth use again.

I go to Los Angeles to see a friend. We smoke. He hires guys to come over. They inject multiple syringes of meth into my veins. He watches while they do this. He calls me Boss. He tells me he loves me. I do not care who does it. I do not care if I overdose. I do not care if the drugs are laced with fentanyl.

Someone else died on me. Why not die on someone else?

I am back in San Francisco. The crash hits like a train.

✢ ✢ ✢

I continue this pattern of dangerously reckless behavior. I surround myself with scary people, the kind who can destroy me. I want this.

I let guys G me out and inject me with whatever is around. I get so high I beg to be destroyed. I do not mean this in some sexual, hard-use way. It is no metaphor. I mean: "Please, just put me down."

I am never able to kill myself or fully commit to putting myself into a situation that ensures my demise. Some cruel survival reflex always kicks in and pulls me back above the raging tide.

After a very close call, I finally tell my boyfriend what is going on.

He lives in Chicago, and we travel back and forth every couple of months. It is the perfect relationship for someone in active addiction. I use all I want. I clean up just enough to see him and act like a sane person.

He is the one good thing I have going on in my life. I fear losing him. I deserve to lose him. I deserve to lose everything.

Please. Please. Just put me down.

SCENE 53

I am in a sling. My hole is being used. What is his name? I don't care — I am flying high. I have been for eight days. My hole gets used — fucked and bred and fisted — every day. And more than once each day.

This is meth sex. This is meth sex for me. I am meth sex. Without it, I am just any other hole. One night only versus eight crazy nights.

Is there even a choice here?

Push the needle. Push the dose. Push the hole. Push out. Push me.

SCENE 54

I am reading an article. It says that meth use may protect against COVID.

I cough as an admin pushes a dose of meth. Is this the vaccine I am waiting for? I am already feeling the effects and my mind dislocates from my body. I turn my head and look at my buddy, a registered nurse.

He prepares his own syringe. I am already blasting off, but he takes his time. Frustratingly so. The high lasts for hours, but the initial rush is short-lived. This is when I am most turned on to play. I really want to take his fist.

He is a self-proclaimed "total fist top." I believe him. I trust him.

He gets between my legs, lubes up his hands. He tries to insert a finger, then two, into my hole. I am too tight. It happens when I am too amped up.

"Relax." I do.

"Do not move." I don't.

He pushes forward with one hand and places his other hand on my stomach, holding me down. I try to help him and wiggle my hole, back and forth, to ease it down the length of his hand. The goal is his wrist, and beyond.

"Dammit, I said don't move." I stop.

He says, "Shut up — do not talk. Follow my lead. Do what I say." His tone is harsh, not smooth or comforting. He pushes. My hole is not ready.

"Fuck. Turn over." I get on all fours.

I am anxious, shaking. My hole is hungry, and I need to be an assertive bottom. He does not like that. He gives me directions that I must follow to the letter.

"You are doing it wrong." The position doesn't work. We move to the sling.

He tries to thrust his fist into me, but I am still too tight. Barely a finger passes through. He is trying to force-fist me, not allowing me to take his fist. This is the wrong way.

I say nothing.

If I make a sound, he glares at me, shuts me up. I do not relax. He does not let up. Forty-five minutes go by. We make no progress.

It is my fault. I know this because he tells me it is.

"You are too high."

"You are a bad bottom."

"Your hole is too tight."

"Have you ever even taken a fist?"

"What's wrong with your body?"

There is no way to trust, to let go, to take his fist. Nothing he says or does is good.

"I am in control."

"Do what I say."

"Do not screw my energy."

"Fuck, dude, what did I just say?"

His ridicule seeps into my brain.

We try again another time. And another. And another. And another.

Each time we meet it is the same. No fist. My fault.

I hope for a different outcome, but the results are always the same.

Am I insane? Or is this part of his kink, his fetish? To get me so high and spun out, and then deny what I crave? To fuck with my mind, locking me in my head, drowning in self-doubt.

I leave his house ashamed, unsatisfied, feeling down about myself. I wonder if I am indeed a bad bottom.

SCENE 55

I show up to his house, again. But this time is different.

Out of the need to please Daddy and to be a good bottom, I decline to slam.

I smoke instead. He is annoyed. I am annoyed. I get high but I moderate my use. Less is more, and I am hell bent on taking his hand today.

I think — I hope — that my initiative and self-control earn approval. They do not. He is visibly irritated. I get it. I usually do not like slamming with someone who isn't also slamming. It creates a weird energy, an imbalance in the way we experience the night.

I insist he slam without me, and he does. I am high and horny for him but calm enough to be worked open.

The same problem resurfaces, yet again. I do not take his hand — on my back, on all fours, or in the sling. But there is something different. I am present. I take any feedback and request Daddy provides.

"Relax." I relax.

"Slow your motions down." I slow down.

Still, no fist. I remain empty, hungry, disheartened. I am aware enough that my perception of reality is true. I know I am doing everything right. Let me do what I do best.

I know my body. I just need to slide the fist in slowly. Then he can punch away at my insides. I like it slow. I like it rough. I like it violent.

"My hands are just too big. They often do not fit into *tight* places," he says, in words laced with irritation and arrogance.

But I am aware in this moment and now I know that his big hands are a barrier only because he makes them a barrier. I know tops who work with me. I know tops who work for me. I know this top is working against me.

He is no co-conspirator in my pleasure. He is a rogue amateur.

It takes numerous sessions to learn the fatal fact: The fetish he presents on the surface lives nowhere inside him. Fisting and chemsex are not his primary fetish. His fetish is control, the denial of pleasure, and the mindfuck of his bottom.

But no more. Without my self-doubt, Daddy resorts to other tactics to explain why his fist is not going in me.

"Your body structure is weird."

"You probably can't take anything up there."

"Your positioning is all wrong."

"You just do not listen."

Finally, he just sits there, his fist firmly in place. No motion. He taunts my hole to take it. I start to move.

"I did not tell you to fucking move, did I?" he spouts, venom and thick saliva dripping off his lips. This goes on for several minutes. My hole reaches out, grabs, tries to suck his fist in. Each time I try he spouts more bile. He conflates being a bottom with being submissive.

A common mistake inexperienced players make.

I leave. My hole is empty and hungry, ravenous even. I do not feel like something is wrong with me.

I know the truth. He is just incompetent.

SCENE 56

It has been seven months. This relapse has stamina. I go back to the nurse's house. Hit replay. I smoke, he slams. Nothing changes. Nothing works. He is a bad top.

Fuck this.

I turn the tables and put him on the bed. I hold his leg down and sit on his foot. In no time, I pass his heal and squeeze his ankle with my asshole.

I know my body. I know my positions. I know my bone structure. I know my hole. Now, I smirk down at him.

I am out. Alpha Bottom status confirmed.

That total top got totally flipped. Give me my trophy, motherfucker.

SCENE 57

The city is half shut down. I don't see the nurse anymore. I am with a different, nameless guy. He prepares the needle, flicking the syringe twice with his finger. There are no bubbles. He hits the vein perfectly. A drop of blood. Wipe.

Good. I am ready.

Wait. Not good.

My jaw is tightening. My teeth click together hard, sending a vibration through my face. They click together again. And again. My teeth begin chattering at a high speed. I look like one of those toys the Joker has in *Batman*.

The dose is way too much. Or it is something else than I thought. This is not the first time.

This is the first time. With this guy. Whoever he is. I am embarrassed. I can't control my mouth. I look to him more than once. He climbs on top of me, using his full weight to pin my movements. This is not the first time. He leans in and whispers in my ear, his stubble scratching my face.

"Stop worrying. This is what I want." I stare at him. He smirks.

I am chemically immobilized. I look at him, annoyed, terrified, my teeth still chattering. He has complete disregard for my physical well-being. I do, too.

I am playing disposable in the context of a scene, yes?

No.

I am living disposable as a human being.

SCENE 58

I drive 10 long hours from San Francisco, my car crammed with
my belongings and my dog. I can't handle the city right now. I am
34 years old, unemployable, and now living with my mother.

I look for jobs. I do not get them. I beat myself up. I am
unworthy. I am worthless.

✣ ✣ ✣

I am meeting a friend of mine in Las Vegas. He is a shaman.
He guides me through a ritual that involves meditation and
consuming tea steeped with psylocibin.

It is an enlightening experience and helps me take a
deeply introspective look into myself. I continue to experiment
with psychedelic and meditation techniques with the goal of
self-exploration.

✣ ✣ ✣

I have a breakthrough on psychedelics, but not during a planned
self-reflective session. It's my sister's birthday, and we take
mushrooms and chill out. We watch *Across the Universe*. We
remember how visual the film is. We do not remember the graphic
violence of the Vietnam War punctuating the beautiful imagery.

My sister is smoking a cigarette on her patio. We hear gunshots coming from the Vegas Strip, just a few miles away. We resume the film but between the gunshots in the movie and the gunshots outside, I need to take my mind off these jolting sounds. I scroll through Facebook.

I learn the gunshots outside are the rubber bullets police have been firing into a crowd of Black Lives Matter protestors on the Strip. Some friends of mine are at the protest and share images and videos of the police assault.

It dawns on me: We are sitting at home high watching a movie, while others are putting their lives on the line to fight for social justice.

Across the Universe ends. I am tripping my ass off with tears streaming down my face wondering what the fuck I've been doing with my life. I have a hard-earned California State Bar license. I have skills. I have passion. I can help.

This is a wake-up call. I can decide to be a victim of myself or get back to helping victims by being an activist.

I need to get a job and get the hell back to San Francisco. Immediately.

SCENE 59

I am sitting in a cold, metal folding chair. We are situated in a circle in some community center, each of us looking nervous, forlorn, bored, scared. This is a 12-step meeting. I have been attending these meetings twice a week for the last couple of months.

I am in hell.

"I have relapsed with crack." Sorry to hear that.

"I have relapsed with alcohol." I understand.

"I have relapsed with meth." Tell me about it.

"I have relapsed with poppers." Wait. What?

My hands are clenched to the sides of my chair, my teeth grinding together, and my legs are squeezed tight. I want to wipe sweat away from my brow, but I am overly conscious about how many times I touch my face.

Sobriety and recovery are not the same thing. One is a state. The other is a process. Don't get it twisted. I consider myself part of the recovery community, and specifically the sober community. I still use poppers; they are not addictive or mind-altering. This is not going to change.

Some people have nicotine. I have poppers.

"I have relapsed, again ... on poppers."

This is the fourth time he's mentioned his poppers relapse this week. I bite my tongue.

+ + +

I am walking out of another meeting, and I feel invigorated. The meeting reunited me with my sponsor, a gay sex worker who empowers me, rather than shutting me or my actions down. We discuss casual sex and the possibility of using plant-based medicine as an alternative for substance use. He is not like other sponsors or people in the 12-step program, who are trained to regurgitate, "you are powerless over all mind-altering substances." This is a set-up for failure. Not every use of every substance leads to misuse or abuse.

I cannot and do not use meth. And, for right now, nothing else either. Meth will always be around. It will always be something I can find or that will find me. But some ways of processing choices in my brain are much easier to consider than others. "I am never allowed to do this" is a lot harder, a lot more tempting for me. I prefer to say: "I can have this, and I am choosing not to."

I am choosing not to.

Pass the poppers, please.

SCENE 60

I have a great weekend with my partner, Sean. *Partner*. I love the sound of it. A brand-new job starts tomorrow. I have a fresh, awesome apartment to set up. A law practice I want to build. And I keep fucking it all up. I have so many good reasons to stay home, but I set the ball in motion to get drunk, so I can justify meth later.

✧ ✧ ✧

I'm high. I feel afraid in my own home. I think my neighbors are watching me. My dog is on edge and her barks freak me out. I am too anxious to go outside. I can't stop sweating.

I put myself in dangerous situations and allow scary people access to my life. I keep replaying my own horror film. In my head. In my life.

I want the thrill, the jump, the rush, the shock.

I am in love with Sean, and I need to show up for him — for us. I get insecure. Who wants a partner on meth? I am in love. He is in love with me. This is a new feeling. This is the fake-out where the monster jumps out. One more scare. I can feel the scene building, hear the low music starting to rumble. The scene is in surround sound. I vibrate with worry.

I reach out to my sponsor because I am the monster. I am hiding from myself. At any moment, I can jump out from the closet and stab me in the back. I can shock me. I can kill me.

The call is coming from inside the house.

SCENE 61

Stephan —

*Please do not go out and use. You have so many
things going well in your life right now. Your career is
taking off, you're captain of the Pedal Pups, you're on
BALIF, you're acting for the first time in the Immortal
Reckoning, and you're getting to work with Peaches.
And we have gotten to a really great place in our
relationship. And you have a great apartment. Using
can jeopardize ALL of that. Keep this a slip-up, please. I
love the fuck out of you, I want to be with you. You can
call me right now. I do not care what time it is or if you
just called two minutes ago. Please let me help.*

I love you,
Sean

PS
See you tomorrow.

SCENE 62

Up for three days. Las Vegas: good. San Francisco: bad —
dangerous. I keep using. I quit work. I quit therapy. I quit caring.

I lie to my family and say I am at the gym. I don't come home
and instead get high in a hotel room with some dude. There is a
rip in my asshole, and I smoke to block the pain. I smoke to make
the pain feel hot. I am used ... up. Used. Up. Used. Up.

I am in my car. I drive, but with no music. Just cold air on
my face.

I look at my phone to find out where I am going.

Where am I going?

Trailer Park. Daddy — tan, leather, hot, dream, nightmare. I
am here. I am not here. I fantasize about him holding me down
with his sweaty arms, his muscles bulging. He blows clouds in my
mouth; holds my mouth to his, forcing his breath into my lungs.
His smoke billows in me. This is my dream.

I do not know this part of town. The sun is setting; I see
headlights. My contacts are dry, my pupils enlarged. Everything is
blurry — blinding. Where is the road?

There are no street signs. There are trailers on the left, right,
and straight ahead. I am surrounded by singlewides. I can't read
the numbers. I am lost. A figure steps out of the darkness. He
points to a spot, and I park. I assume this is who I am meeting.

He is no Daddy — no tan, no leather, no muscles. He is old and wrinkly, missing teeth and wearing cheap pleather chaps. He is high as fuck. There are no bright lights in the trailer — thankfully. Trash is everywhere; chunks of walls are missing. The trailer is a mess. He is a mess. This is not a dream sequence. It looks more like a crime scene.

I can work with this. I need more of the high.

✛ ✛ ✛

After scoping out the living room, I finally settle in on the couch. He hands me a pipe and asks if I have supplies. I reach for the torch in my vest. I smoke his pipe, which tastes like plastic. I try to suck his dick. It is flaccid. No problem. He has two hands. I let him finger my hole with his dirty nails. No lube, but I am high and determined. He keeps squirming around, so I tell him to get on his back and be still. I take off his boot to reveal his crusty toenails. I spit on his foot and grind it into my hole. This seems to freak him out. He asks for a break. He asks to slow down. I am here to get higher and fuck harder. I want to rev up, but he's pumping the breaks.

He asks about my tattoos. I'm irritated. I pull out my phone to find my next trick. "This tattoo is Lady Gaga's signature," I point out. A car rumbles down the drive.

He looks for Gaga videos. I look for a trick. His Wi-Fi connection is weak. More rumbling. Someone is approaching. He says his roommate is home but there is only one room.

+ + +

I am getting high with a stranger who has lied about everything. My instincts are firing on overdrive. I tell him I am going to go meet my dealer and get more stuff. I pull up my pants, zip up my boots, and hold my keys so that the metal teeth poke aggressively through my knuckles.

I make it to my car and promptly lock the doors. But it is hot, so I lower the driver's side window. The road splits, and I ask him which is the way out. He tells me to go right. This is a lie. I went down that road when searching for his place. It leads to a dark end. I look down it and see a lone car with its parking lights on. Someone is waiting. I take the left turn instead. The car starts to follow me.

I speed through the trailer park and tear onto the main street. It is black outside. No streetlights, just headlights. I am so blinded by the lights that I can barely see the lines on the road. I see a gas station ahead and decide to pull in. I try to calm down. I open the apps. I need a trophy.

I am too high to get out of the car. I cannot even pretend to pump gas, just to get some air. I sit there, and the car pulls behind me. The lights are blinding. The car does not move. Nobody gets out. It just waits.

I am high. I am spooked. What is real? I start up my car and begin to pull out. The car follows. I do a circle around the parking lot and pull into one of the well-lit parking spots in front of the station's market. The car parks at a pump directly behind me again. Bright headlights beaming on me, through me.

✢ ✢ ✢

I am sweating, panicking. I cannot drive away from this. I can barely see. Lights are coming at me. Lights coming for me. Where do I run?

An ambulance pulls in on the left, perpendicular to my car, the lights shining directly in my face. The headlights from behind bounce from every mirror. My eyes dart, bounce, roll. Somebody is going to get me.

There is no more running. I am trapped. By paranoia, by a predator. I am trapped. I cannot move.

I call my dad. I ask him to pick me up. He is in the middle of Rosh Hashanah seder with my entire family. He tells me he will come and hangs up the phone.

A few seconds later, my aunt calls. Instead, she will pick me up. I tell her I am in danger. I tell her people are following me. I tell her that I am afraid.

She says my sister will ride with her and then drive my car home. I send my location. It will take ten minutes to get to me. I am terrified. The car is still behind me, headlights on. I ask my aunt to stay on the phone until she finds me. She does. I do not know what we talk about.

My eyes continue to dart — left, right, center; left, right, center. The ambulance finally pulls away. I have been here for more than 30 minutes.

Eternity falls around me, and my aunt pulls in. My sister gets out, hugs me, takes my keys, and hops behind the wheel of my car. I dart into my aunt's passenger seat. As we both pull out of the station, we drive past the car behind me at the pump.

There is no one inside.

✢ ✢ ✢

I am crashing Rosh Hashanah seder after being gone for several days. I panic. My entire family will be there. I tell my aunt I am scared.

We pull into the driveway. She says she loves me. I pause before I reach the front door. She gives me a long hug and reminds me, "Everyone on the other side of that door loves you." She tells me not to be scared of being loved by them. I am terrified. I am ashamed. I look and feel like shit. I am crashing. I have crashed.

I walk through the front door and head directly into the spare bedroom, making sure to avoid eye contact with everyone. I collapse onto the bed. A few minutes later, my aunt knocks on the door. She has a glass of juice and a plate of food for me. She puts it on the bedside table, leaves the room, and quietly closes the door.

It is dark in here now. It is dark where I am.

SCENE 63

I am listening to the album, *Make It Big*, by Wham! I am dancing around my room to "Careless Whisper."

My mother has been brainwashing me from the time that I was very little to love 80's music. I was born in 1987. My mother was 20 years old at the time and she grew up with Depeche Mode, Duran Duran, Queen, New Order, The B-52's, and the like. Out of this immersion in 80s music culture came my love, adoration, and solid obsession with George Michael.

✦ ✦ ✦

In 1998, George Michael's bop-pop image shatters in a bathroom stall.

I am 10 years old when George Michael is arrested for "lewd acts" in a Los Angeles public restroom. I am much too young to understand what "lewd acts" are, and I am many years away from discovering the magic and cultural significance for gay men behind public cruising and sex.

It takes until adulthood for me to realize how much of a gay activist George Michael really was.

After his arrest in Will Rogers Memorial Park, George Michael never apologizes for his behavior. He says there was nothing inherently wrong with what he did. Six months later, he appears on the *Late Show with David Letterman* to discuss the arrest. Courageously, George casts the police officer who entrapped him as the villain in the situation — not his own sexuality or behavior. He uses wit, humor, and charm to call out stigma around gay men's sexuality.

"I've been told backstage I couldn't say the 'M' word. So, god knows, if you're not allowed to say it, no wonder I got arrested doing it." The "M" word is masturbation, which George eventually says out loud on camera, to great audience applause.

Instead of his appearance on the *Late Show* being a one-time statement, George becomes a crusader against police entrapment and a critic of society for criminalizing and shaming his sexuality.

He becomes a defiant gay icon, speaking transparently about his love of sex and cruising.

He tells one interviewer: "Gay people in the media are doing what makes straight people comfortable, and automatically my response to that is to say I'm a dirty filthy fucker and if you can't deal with it, you can't deal with it."

During his appearances and interviews, George Michael is more concerned about looking fat in his arrest photo than people knowing he is a cruising faggot. Instead of burying his arrest, he leans heavy into its energy. He is a sexual rebel.

I realize I relate to him on a level that goes much deeper than his music.

George Michael releases his next single, "Outside," a track sampling radio reports of his arrest. The music video is filmed less than two months after the arrest, featuring both gay and straight couples fucking in public, being caught on camera, and subsequently, accosted by the police. Throughout the action and arrests, George appears dressed as an LAPD officer dancing in front of a wall of urinals in a public bathroom. It is decked out with disco balls.

I think it's important that I can be out there and say
that I'm a big tart and still have a big smash album.
When I was tempted to give up in the middle of making

this album, one of the things that made that difficult for me is that I would have felt I'd have let down a whole generation of young gay kids. That they'd think 'he's massive, then he comes out and then he's gone.' When I made the 'Outside' video I knew I was helping a whole generation of 15-year-olds who are cruising and dying of shame about it. I felt that lightening the stigma around cruising was the most immediately beneficial thing I could do. I know for a fact that when I was 16, 17, when I started cruising, that watching the 'Outside' video would have taken some of the weight off my shoulders.

George Michael, 1998

George Michael is a sexual outlaw. I am made in his image.

SCENE 64

I do not realize how much my HIV status weighs me
down until the U=U study concludes that "undetectable
equals untransmittable."

> *Being undetectable means that the virus [HIV] is*
> *less able to attack your immune system cells ...*
> *People who are undetectable do not transmit HIV*
> *to other people through sex.*

> San Francisco AIDS Foundation

Once I hear this news, I am finally realizing how broken my
HIV diagnosis has left me. I was so close to getting that damn
biohazard tattoo, to bearing an external mark and showing the
world that my blood was toxic. It would be easier for me to
broadcast it to everyone with a tattoo — to take away the power
from some stranger cruelly repeating to me what I already know.
How I already feel: toxic and broken.

U=U reframes how I see myself. I no longer see the need to
physically label myself with a literal biohazard warning. I have HIV,
but the knowledge of U=U transforms my status from a deadly
toxicity into something like a new blood type — not a systemic
flow of shame rushing through my veins.

I am neither toxic nor broken.

I am going to be okay.

SCENE 65

SESTA-FOSTA, a bipartisan bill claims to stop sex trafficking.
It does not. SESTA-FOSTA stands for the Stop Enabling Sex
Trafficking Act and the Fight Online Sex Trafficking Act, but it
is just a scare tactic for control, like Proposition 60. Somebody
always needs protecting from life's most natural act: sex. In
reality, the bill does nothing for trafficking except make it harder
to find. The bill eliminates the trackable online mechanisms
that sex traffickers use, along with a wide variety of other
non-exploitive sexual expression, community connection, and
grassroots education. This is not progress. Nobody is safer.
Because of SESTA-FOSTA, the definition of "sex trafficking" now
encompasses all sex work, coerced and consensual.

Politicians smile. Sex workers suffer. Traffickers hide.

Let's kill all the lawyers.

✛ ✛ ✛

Viral Loads pays no royalties to me. No porn does, when a studio is involved. Fan sites, such as JustFor.Fans, finally allow performers to be paid like other entertainment professionals. I can finally be paid for each time somebody watches me take a load or give a fist. Fan sites are the democratization of porn. Everyone now has access to a piece of the porn pie.

Everyone has access to a piece of my porn pie.

✢ ✢ ✢

Fantasies are now considered reality. A rape scene is regulated and prohibited as if actual rape. Sex showing alcohol or drugs is prohibited. It is the same old prohibition just in a narrower context. I am not allowed to consent to a rape scene or a drug slamming scene. I am not allowed to be hypnotized in a scene, even with my legal permission. This is the policing of fantasy.

Others — not sure who, specifically — cannot see me do what I want to do with my own body. I have no choice. I am produced for mass consumption.

I am a sexual outlaw. I hope that in an age ruled by the sex police I stay a sexual outlaw. These days, the outlaws are heroes. We fight for your right to fuck however you want: naturally, brutally, high, hypnotically.

My body is not here to be censored. I express myself freely. It's my right. My asshole is protected by the First Amendment. My sex is transgressive. My sex is political. My sex will never be a banned book.

SCENE 66

I am not going back to work at a law firm. If I do there will be zero life balance. My hard work will only benefit someone else. This is a recipe for relapse.

I take a hard look at what sort of life I want for myself. The people I most admire marry their personal passions with their work. I want that. I will not silo myself anymore; I will not give into the sickness and addiction of assimilation. I will not erase me — any of me. I am here to make a positive impact on queer and kinky people's lives. I am here to serve the sexual outlaws who are my brothers, my sisters, my siblings, my community.

I open the Law Office of Stephan F. Ferris.

✦ ✦ ✦

It takes almost nine months to get the wind under my wings, but I do. My practice focuses on adult entertainment and queer businesses.

It pays to be an outlaw — politically, emotionally, sexually.
I am going to be okay. I want us to all be okay.

SCENE 67

Ninety days.

I am now a member of The Stonewall Project, a state-certified drug and alcohol treatment program that is managed by the San Francisco AIDS Foundation and is available to gay, bi, queer, and trans men. It provides harm-reduction-based counseling, which encompasses substance use, mental health, sexuality, HIV / STI prevention, and education services.

This program meets people where they currently are in their recovery and sobriety. They place harm reduction into three separate phases. *Total abstinence*, which can be achieved without membership or the participation in any particular program. *Targeted abstinence*, which focuses on stopping use of a particular substance, or combination of substances. And, *controlled / safer use*, which requires the taking of extra precautions around chemical use, and it can exist in a targeted abstinence framework. This method allows someone to consider or explore healthier ways to use a chemical, such as using test kits and clean syringes. We work for "progress not perfection." Recovery is not binary. It is neither "in" nor "out." It is neither "good" nor "bad." Recovery is not moral. It is a process.

I now ask myself whether using a substance *adds* or *subtracts* from my current momentum or energy, and how it might impact my short-term goals and long-term goals.

Am I sacrificing long-term joy for short-term gratification?

I enter the next stage of my recovery.

I am going to be okay.

SCENE 68

Everything is set — towels, tissues, tourniquet, syringe.

I am home alone. I push the *play* button. The fun begins.

The guys in the video tie blue bands around their biceps. They each insert a syringe into their own veins. It takes about 30 seconds for them to empty their syringes. The bands come off; the tissues are applied. The guys fuck.

My tongue runs across my lips, a reflexive response to the porn I am watching. This is how I get my fix now. I no longer trust myself at parties with guys slamming right in front of me. I no longer show up at the gambler's table. I no longer risk complete bankruptcy.

A fetish is a need or desire for an object, body part, setting, or activity for excitement. My fetish is a part of me. It is a switch that has been turned on that cannot be turned off. Slamming remains my fetish — my obsession. It includes the ritual of doing it and the guys performing the ritual. It excites me, and that exists both with and without the sex; even if the sex itself includes other fetishes — hands, rope, feet, leather, piss, shit, cum. Like my sexuality and my queerness, my fetish is not a choice. It is in me. Slamming is in me. No needle necessary.

An entire porn genre exists for people like me. From studio-produced fantasies of slamming and chemsex, to homemade videos on the web, to dedicated porn sites.

I need the "money shot." I need to witness the actual register, and slamming, smoking, or other methods of ingesting the chemicals. I need to see the plume of red.

These scenes allow me — sober me — to directly engage in a meth sex fantasy without directly using. I engage in the fetish by jerking off to it, safely at home. These men — these slam pigs — cannot entice me to come over and play.

Please be kind. Rewind.

SCENE 69

Are you a cop? Are you here to record and tattle? Are you one of us?

　Let's blow clouds.

I am in a Zoom room for chemsex fetishists. Right now, 17 of us are in various stages of smoking, slamming, jerking, fucking, or watching. The room's resident DJ plays music, creating the perfect dark, moody scene preferred for chemsex. All of the open, stacked windows on the screen look like a Brady Bunch-style collection of sex fiends.

Here, I engage with men who play and fuck, but who mostly show off their smoking and slamming skills. I have direct access to my favorite ritual, to actual use. Nothing is sanitized by a studio or website. These men do it for me, and that does it for me.

Clouds are blown front and center to the camera. I watch the slam ritual happen in real time. These communities organize and share video conference links back and forth on various social media. A little cross-referencing, and I find yet more custom, niche rooms: Dad / son fetishists that party; foot / sneaker fetishists that party; piss fetishists that party. The list goes on and on in every imaginable way.

I am a voyeur. I do not want to use with my community, but I want to be a part of my community of chemsex fetishists. Just like being in a room full of guys slamming, there is an element of risk. I know I am on the tip of the point.

There is an explicit rule: Cameras stay on. This space is for PNP fetishists to connect. It is a risk to invite new people. We share vulnerable information, and that risk needs to be shared by all. Occasionally, announcements are made in the group chat to actively share that risk. Sometimes they ask for everyone to blow a cloud at the same time, or to show off their paraphernalia, or to start prepping a rig.

✦ ✦ ✦

I am anxious. I know these guys. A dark cloud sits above me the entire time I am in the chat. I watch other guys blow smoke or slam. I await the group call for everyone to participate. I worry I will get kicked out if I don't use on cue. This is my haven, my safe space. I am present with men slamming. I am also present with myself. I am safe.

I want to participate in my fetish without participating in the use. This isn't one-sided, like with a video. It is live and my brothers in this ritual want some sort of interaction back from me.

"Alright! Everyone, blow a cloud!"

Shit. What's the point?

SCENE 70

I enter a house where the host has invited several guys for a full night of fucking, breeding, pissing, fisting, and whatever else may capture us. I recognize most of them from playing together before, from staying up for days. All of the guys are slamming tonight.

I am still sober, but resisting the drugs becomes increasingly difficult. My experience as a sober participant is losing its luster.

Being from Las Vegas, I am a born gambler. Tonight is high stakes. I might make it out okay. I might fall into the trap I set for myself.

I do not need to gamble with money. Drugs remain my coin, my slot machine, my roulette wheel, my game of chance. Russian roulette, 007 style.

✢ ✢ ✢

I watch guys prepare the syringes. I watch the drugs drain into dusty veins. I see eyes roll back, heavy lids closing; they flutter.

This is too much. The thirst is begging for its water. I imagine the blackness of my pupils is fully consuming the blue of my eyes. I feel my arm turn, exposing my empty veins. They plea for mercy, for relieving the want. I act as if on autopilot, knowing the route to oblivion.

No. I abort the desire and take off. There is no high flying without a crash landing.

I try to play, hyperaware of my surroundings. I am the only guy not high. Anxiety seeps in. There is no way to fuck or to fist. I flee. I fly. But I do not fly away into the dark water of the black sea inside. This is neither a win nor a loss.

It is a draw. Every gambler knows: Eventually, luck runs out. I live not on if, but when. When will the thirst override my mind? When will the tank of my body or spirit be completely empty? When will my veins take to their long, syrupy drink, gulping to fill what is always gone?

SCENE 71

I am wearing the gray Bike brand shorts Sean gave me for Hanukkah. I pair them with a SuperTwunk tank that says, "Cum Dump." I drive down the freeway with the windows down, blasting the new *Slut Pop* album by Kim Petras.

San Diego isn't as warm as I thought it would be.

I keep the heat on to keep my legs from shivering. There are three loads in me already this morning. Different guys. Different apartments. I took 30 dicks last night at the Wallbanger party.

I have no idea if they were different dicks or repeats. I am still insatiably horny.

This morning's hat trick isn't doing it for me, though; three loads isn't enough. I am just getting warmed up. I want more. I need more. To keep going. Fuck. Rinse. Repeat. Skip the rinsing. I decline any offer to take a shower once bred. I simply pull up my blue jock and my shorts and leave. On to the next one, covered in sweat and cum. I sniff myself. I am ripe and it turns me on. Each conquest is a kick of adrenaline, and I can't calm down. Each load ramps me up. This elevated state will last until I cum. Until then, I am bottomless.

I am almost six-months sober. I fire up Sniffies to find my next trophy. One profile catches my immediate attention: a single circled profile filled with white smoke. The smoke is mesmerizing. I know exactly what this means. If I am feeling this, I shouldn't be on Sniffies.

Disengaging from Sniffies is part of my recovery strategy, specifically my strategy for this weekend trip. Before leaving home, my partner and I plan on how to keep me sober. I decide no hookup apps.

He is scared. I am scared.

I salivate when I see sketchy boys on sketchy apps. I know this about myself. The pattern repeats so many times that I cannot ignore it. It is ingrained. I am Pavlov's dog, drool and all.

I am breaking the rules with Sniffies. And I am already gravitating toward white clouds and diamond emojis. My brothers and I know how to signal what we want.

I can say no, but I keep looking for the codes, the signals. Something is pulling at me from beneath the surface. I do not want to use. I very much want to use.

I am confused. I am consumed.

I miss the sketchiness. I miss running around town at all hours of the night. I miss playing uninhibitedly. I miss fucking for days.

✢ ✢ ✢

I can't stop looking at the white smoke. Last time in San Diego, I used for days. I did not return home when I told Sean I would. He worried. He watched my dog. He is watching my dog right now while I am here, while I am cruising trashy boys on Sniffies. In between messages, I see cute videos that Sean sends with Daenerys, snuggling together. He calls me.

"Hi, Baby Boy. How's your day going?"

"It is fine."

"What're you up to?"

"Getting a load. Can I call you later?"

"Who's the lucky guy?"

"Some dude off Sniffies."

I do not lie. His tone changes. He goes quiet. He is upset. He tells me to call him after. He doesn't want to talk now, but there will be a long conversation later. I say, "Okay."

I tell him I have to go.

✢ ✢ ✢

I am chatting with a guy who's been up for three days. He sends me his address. He has a big dick in his profile, but I notice several pictures with his ass up in the air. I tell him that I am a bottom. He asks if I party. I say I have but not yet today. It is not a lie. It is not true either.

I need to know that I am going to get fucked. I tell him that I do not top. I tell him that I want him to add his load to the three already inside me. I am very direct about what I am looking for. At least I think I am. He promises to breed me. I tell him I am on my way. I tell him that I want him to blow a huge cloud on my cock when I get there. I repeat that I am a bottom.

I ask if he has any videos of him partying. He doesn't.

It takes 15 minutes to get to his apartment. It should be 10, but I miss his exit twice. I am nervous. I am not paying attention to Google Maps. He lives far from Hillcrest, in a shabby white industrial building.

I realize he forgot to give me his apartment number. Typical tweaker mistake. Maybe I did not ask, knowing that it would slow me down. Maybe something inside me is pulling me away from this. I message on Sniffies, asking for the apartment number. Fifteen more minutes pass. White clouds roll through my mind, a thunderhead, a coming storm. I am stirring. But he is not responding. My anxiety takes over. I pull back onto the road and return to Hillcrest, preparing myself for an unpleasant phone call with Sean. I am not ready to tell him how close I just came. A part of me wishes he sent a complete address. A part of me is grateful he did not.

I am sad. I feel ashamed, broken, weak, and left out.

I am cold and miserable. San Diego isn't as warm as I thought it would be.

SCENE 72

I am in First Congregational Church looking for a place called "Barnum." It is just before 11 a.m., and the white halls of the church reflect sunshine that beams through large double-paned windows. It is a warm morning, and it is going to be a dangerously hot day. I wore a tee-shirt, but I should have chosen a tank. I am already sweaty. I make my way through the crowded hallways filled with gay men.

I am attending a workshop called "Cross the Line." It is the second workshop on the second day of a weekend conference for crystal meth addicts.

I go to meetings like this because I like being a part of a community. I like having extra accountability. I am hoping to connect with other sober gay guys at this conference. Maybe even get a couple sober loads in this church. They say you can't smoke a pipe with a dick in your mouth. That's not entirely true, but I admire the sentiment behind it. I am very much a pro-ho reformed methhead.

I finally see a sign for Barnum. It is a large room at the end of one of the hallways. I enter and take a seat next to a young woman from San José. She is trans and it is also her first time at this conference. She is newly in recovery. We keep chatting as the room fills up. Then the room quiets as a man steps to the front and introduces himself. I do not catch his name, so I glance down at my program. There is no panel description, just the words "Cross the Line," the time, and the presenters' names. There are two listed for this workshop. He must be either "Lee M." or "Mike L."

Lee or Mike point to the back of the room and direct the audience to look at a line of blue painter's tape stuck to the floor. The line divides the room in half. It turns out this panel is not a panel at all. It is an interactive workshop with rules. Lee or Mike explain that everyone starts on one side of the line until a question is asked. If the answer to the question is "yes," then you step across the line. Each person can interpret the questions however they choose, and every answer is personal and subjective. The intent of this exercise is to find commonality with the other people who cross the line with you. They instruct us to leave our seats.

I find my place behind the line of tape. The first set of questions are straightforward.

"Cross the line if you wear contact lenses or glasses."

"Cross the line if you live outside of Los Angeles."

"Cross the line if you have an addiction to drugs or alcohol."

I cross the line each time. The next set of questions start getting a bit heavier.

"Cross the line if you have ever blown off friends to do drugs."

"Cross the line if you have lied to a family member about doing drugs."

"Cross the line if you have ever driven a car drunk or high."

I cross the line each time. The prompts continue to get darker and more difficult.

"Cross the line if you have ever been hospitalized for your drug or alcohol use."

"Cross the line if you have ever been violent while on drugs or alcohol."

"Cross the line if someone has overdosed and you've continued to use just after."

I cross the line.

I cross the line.

I cross the line.

SCENE 73

I almost slip as I rush to get into the shower. It is 2:35 p.m. and I have exactly 25 minutes to clean out and get dressed. That leaves me 30 minutes to get from Koreatown to West Hollywood. Google says it should only take 27 minutes. My morning cleanout was thorough, so this should just be a quick touch-up.

I am anxious. It is not because I am in a hurry. I am anxious because I am feeling insecure. The guy I am driving to is a fucking Adonis. He is dreamy. He is gorgeous. He wants to film with me. I do not want to face rejection.

I dry off and pull on my black jeans. They fit tight. I have barely trained for AIDS / LifeCycle, and I have been eating garbage all weekend. I should just cancel. I can make up some random excuse. Maybe I say that my stomach isn't cooperating? Nobody wants to film with that guy. It's too late to say I have COVID. I just need to cancel. I need to buy more time to work out and show up looking more like my pictures. I feel good about the pictures I sent. They are only two weeks old. But right now, there's a disconnect between how I feel in the photographs and how I feel in my head.

No, I can't cancel. I have already delayed the shoot a day. If I cancel now, he will think I am a flake. He will never want to fuck me.

I suck it up. I do 20 push-ups and I text him. I am on my way. It takes 17 minutes longer than Google estimated, but I find easy parking. He greets me at the door.

He is even more beautiful in person than he is on Instagram. Curly red hair. Stunning blue eyes. And pits that reek of testosterone. He pours me a glass of water and leads me to his bedroom. I take off my shoes and sunglasses and place them in the corner as he sets up three cameras. One on a tripod. One on his dresser. One mounted to the ceiling fan.

He hits record on two of the cameras, and then uses his Apple Watch to get the third rolling. We start by making out. Then, he pushes me over onto the bed, my face down onto a pillow. He fucks me hard. He fucks me how I like.

I am in awe, and I am happy my head is in the pillow. It allows me to hide my face, so I do not look stupid in his eyes. It allows me to enjoy the moment without acting or playing anything up for the camera. The pillow is long enough to cover my stomach, to hide my worry and conceal my fat-kid shame. I feel so out of place and disgusting right next to this porn god.

Fifteen minutes into fucking and I beg for him to cum in me. I do not want his load just yet. This is a panic response. I am so overwhelmed and in my head that I want this moment to be over. He thrusts harder and his moans build to orgasm. He has not ejaculated, but it is a brilliant performance. I appreciate him reading my cue of wanting to wrap this up. Some tops do not, and they take forever to cum. This is a scene. This scene is over.

We stop the cameras, and I dress. I thank him for having me over and apologize for acting like a fanboy. He tells me he had fun, but I do not believe it. He is just being polite. He tells me that he is happy we got to connect and film. He says he is being increasingly selective about who he films with. He tells me that he can't film without chemistry. I think to myself: He is really going for the Oscar here.

I tie my shoes but before I leave, he asks to take a picture to share on social media. We take one with a smile. Then another making out. Then a video making out. Standard promo material. I can't wipe the dumbstruck look off my face. I can't wait to get out the front door, so I stop embarrassing myself.

I take a big sip of the glass of water on the table. He is rubbing his dick through his gym shorts. It is still hard from his Trimix injection. He didn't get off earlier, so he asks if I would like to go back to his room and play some more — off camera. I am in shock. A wave of relief floods my body and my anxiety calms.

I kick off my sneakers and pull down my shorts.

I am going to be okay.

SCENE 74

"I'm sorry, but it's getting late. I'm heading out." It is almost midnight. That means I should go home and not seek out guys for sex tonight. If I continue to look for cock after midnight, the chances of me being offered drugs increases exponentially.

Call me a gremlin — never feed me after midnight. Or just consider me Cinderella — when the clock strikes twelve, I dip out fast.

✢ ✢ ✢

"Hey, I'm taking loads at this dude's place tonight. It's at —— ."

"Have fun!"

"I'll check back in with you in an hour to let you know I'm okay."

I am walking into a fifth-floor apartment. The occupant is
to wreck my hole. At times like this — when I'm feeling squirrely —
I text my partner or my sponsor for accountability. The "buddy
system" can work wonders when in recovery, or just meeting
someone new. I use this system when escorting, and it is a
great safety tool. I also turn off the face and fingerprint
identification on my phone before I meet a stranger for sex —
six digit passcode only.

Dead hookers still have fingerprints.

✛ ✛ ✛

I no longer use hook-up apps. No more Grindr. No more Scruff.
No more Sniffies. Nothing. It is too easy for meth to find me in
these digital bathhouses.

✛ ✛ ✛

It is summer. I am in Buena Vista Park. It is after dusk. I find my
parking spot at the top of the hill and make my way down the
familiar, secluded shelf. It is warm, with a soft, cooling breeze. The
park is magical on this kind of night.

It is also terrifying. It is completely dark, so I can't see
anything. It's creepy. I like it. The moving shadows are something

straight out of a horror movie. It's hot as fuck. It makes my dick pulse. Do not be surprised if I end up dead in some park one day.

I hope I have one final, fun fuck.

SCENE 75

S: Let's fuck again sometime. U around tonight? Can host.

J: R u at gym?

S: Nah. Just got home.

J: Ok. R u up late? I may be available tonight but not till late evening ... no meth. Pls confirm.

S: Yes. No meth here either. Glad u said that :)

J: Great.

S: I'll just be working around the house. How late you thinkin?

J: Like, after 11 if tonight.

S: Perfect. Can ya send some pics? Unshowered and musky is preferable.

J: Mmmm. Yum.

S: Loved sniffing my ass on ur fingers while I was sucking u last time.

J: FUCK YES. Hang on. Will send pics later. You're giving
me a raging hard on at the gym.

S: Fuck yeah pig ... would love to get ya in my rim chair.

J: I'll be sure to be stanky.

S: Sexy ffucker. What do ya get into?

J: More top quite raunchy.

S: Total raunch pig here.

J: I have a dinner to attend, and can check in a few hours ...
I am still hard, toilet pig.

S: See ya then.

SCENE 76

I am with my old sponsor in his hotel room. We do not work the
steps together anymore, but we are still good friends. I see him
at least every two or three weeks when I get my hair faded. It
is Thanksgiving weekend, and we are both in town for a big sex
party in Los Angeles. I am on a budget and crashing with a friend
who lives not too far away in Koreatown. My former sponsor is
staying at the host hotel, which is home to Horse Market, the party
I am most excited for. It is an evening where men are divided into

stallions and mares. The entire point is insemination, and not artificial like in some stables.

I arrive in Los Angeles, and I roam the hotel. I do a few loops through the vendor mart, and then make my way through a few boys' hotel rooms.

Horse Market has a strict call time for bottoms. I need to arrive — cleaned out and ready to go — by 6 p.m., or a little bit earlier if I want to secure a good spot. There are only a limited number of mare tickets available, and they tend to sell out quickly. In this party, the mares arrive early and check their clothes. They get into a sling or on a fuck bench. Then, just before the party opens to stallions, the mares are hooded. The stallions enter and fuck as they desire. White hoods signify condoms. Red hoods signify natural. Again, for me, red means go — hard.

Mares want this wild, free breeding so badly that tickets are released by lottery. As always, prized semen is in high demand. The bloodlines are what counts.

Give me my trophy.

After I check in, I hand over my clothes to a cute attendant. He gives me an iPad with a legal form to review and sign. I know this form. I am the lawyer who drafted it.

In a jock, with my poppers in the waist band, my nervousness kicks in. Will enough guys fuck me? Will I hold up okay? What about cravings? Normally I take a hit off my vape pen and do a dose of GHB just before arriving. Not this time. This time I am relying solely on my poppers and my will to make it through the event. This is something I need to do. I need to prove to myself I can cross this line, pass this bar.

I claim one of the slings. It is not in the center but off to the side. It is not prime real estate, but it will do. Some of the other mares get stuck with a fuck bench. For me, stamina requires a sling. I eliminate as much worry as possible and settle in.

We are about to start. Volunteers come through with hoods. There are no white ones. A helpful stable hand comes to me and delicately places the hood over my head, rolling the bottom part up to reveal only my lips. He ties the hood in the back and helps me get into the sling. I hear my friend's voice. He runs the event and explains the tops are ready to do their work. He opens the gates.

Blindfolded and waiting, bottoms have no sense of time during Horse Market. I want a trackable goal in my mind, but that is not possible here. I am just a hole, floating and beyond time.

I hear the guy to my left get fucked. And then some guy across the room. I am afraid no one will fuck me. That I'll be forced to sit in my sling, empty, humiliated. Then, some random stallion wanders over and falls into my hole. And then another. And then another.

+ + +

Seventeen guys breed me, back-to-back. It has been 15 minutes; it has been two hours — I do not know. I do not care.

I take loads until I am satisfied and ready to leave. Still blindfolded and in the sling, I raise my right hand over my head, a familiar but now benign gesture. A stable hand comes to ask if I am okay. He is here to take care of me. I tell him I am ready to head out and he helps me up, placing both of my hands on his shoulders. I have to remain blindfolded while in the play area to protect the integrity of anonymity — under no circumstances are mares allowed to see stallions. He asks me to walk slowly and leads me out of the play area.

Once outside, I feel defeated. Maybe I should have stayed? I want to go further, to last longer, to take more.

I go to the elevators. I start cruising the hallways.

SCENE 77

I sit down at my desk to write. It is 3:33 p.m. There is no legal work to do. The first draft of my manuscript is nearly complete but there is still more work ahead. One day left to deadline. Then that's it — no more of this story.

Pressure mounts on several fronts. On a nearby notepad reads my To-Do List:

Finish the book!

Record for the podcast.

Post videos.

I also have to focus on raising money for AIDS / LifeCycle. I am team captain. My goal this year is $25,000 and I am so close. My personal best so far has been $18,000. I am on the fundraising leaderboard: Top 50! I can sustain. I will sustain.

This is all on the side — this stuff that makes life work now.

I run a law practice. I pay my rent. I pay my bills. But not much more. It is stressful, and I need to get ahead. My attorney friends are thriving. My sex worker friends are thriving. I am stuck in the middle. I worry. When will clients pay?

I have good experiences. I have bad experiences. Things take me longer. I lose track. I lose the thread. I lose out. I have a hard time focusing. Still no ADHD meds from my psychiatrist because of my substance history. He will not treat me. He punishes me for where I have been rather than supporting where I am going.

No time for that. Push through this, like everything else.

Please focus, Stephan. Please.

Phone buzzing. Facebook notification. I am in debt. Who's competing at IML? I miss Darklands. What's next? I have to write.

Please focus, Stephan. Please.

Why did I even go to law school? Why did I think I could do this? Scroll TikTok. Fucking psychiatrist. Just write, you asshole.

Please just write. Please focus, Stephan. Please.

I grab a La Croix. It is *pastèque*, watermelon in French. Four years in high school and another two in college. I am what the French call *les incompetents*, the incompetent ones. I scroll. I see a meme. *Listen lady, let me tell you what mansplaining means.* I laugh. I identify with the incompetent ones. But I am not incompetent. I am not stupid. Merely distracted. I need to write.

Please focus, Stephan. Please.

Daenerys rests on my bed. She is under the sheet, her paw out, her head on a pillow. A little being, looking back at me. She must be accustomed to me making such a commotion all the time. Still, she loves me.

I crawl in bed with her. I pull her body close to mine and put my arms around her. I make her the little spoon. I set an alarm and take a quick nap. I dream I'm hosting a drag show. Daenerys is providing commentary in the confessional cutaways. I don't know what it means, but I wake well-rested.

I am awake. I focus. I sit down at my desk to write. And I write:

I am going to be okay.

I am going to be okay.

I am going to be okay.

Acknowledgments

As someone who needs many projects and distractions to maintain some semblance of sanity and sobriety, I tend to move through life experiences quickly. It has taken a lot (an entire pandemic) for me to slow down and learn to be present, to savor joy, and to sit with uncomfortable emotions. Writing this book has allowed me the opportunity to revisit and examine parts of myself and my life that I either turned a blind eye to or simply moved through too quickly to process. Thank you, Patrick Davis, for providing me with this incredible form of therapy, your constant encouragement, and your kind expertise as a publisher and editor. Cory Firestine, your editorial support and flexibility made sure this book made it on press, on time. Thank you, also, to Amariah Love, MS, NCC, LPC, for her sensitivity review and advice on the difficult content in this book. I also appreciate the focused work and care of Raymond Luczak in preparing my manuscript for publication.

I don't think I would be alive today, except for my partner's compassion and endless support. Every time I slipped and stumbled, Sean stuck around to help me get back on my feet. He provided love when I could not provide love for myself. For the longest time, I could not envision a future. I thought I had achieved everything I needed to achieve; I was content to fade away. Now, I'm excited to dream again and build a future — for myself and with Sean. He encourages me to be a better person, take smart risks, and keep growing. I love you so much, Baby Boy.

I am incredibly grateful and privileged to be raised by parents that are accepting of my queerness and sexuality. I have never had to question if my mom and dad love me, and they've always been supportive of me creating my own journey. My dad, Al, has always trusted me to make decisions for myself and treated me with dignity. My mom, Tosca, has been a great teacher of compassion and an enormous influence on my taste in art and music. As much as my ego hated to come home and move in with my parents, I'm so happy for the time that we've spent together.

To my oldest sister Taylor: I am thrilled you have found your way back home. It's exciting to watch you grow into a powerful and loving queer woman. I absolutely loved going to the Drag Race finale with you, and I look forward to watching you build your life with Terryn.

To my youngest sister, Peytan: You are the backbone of our family, and I admire what you sacrifice and endure to keep us afloat. I have the greatest respect for how hard you work to better yourself and our family. Plus, I love that you're an even bigger fangirl than I am about pop music.

To my youngest brother, Evan: Based on looks, we could be twins, though we lead very different lives. I love that we share a passion for media and that when we are together, we can geek out over *Marvel* and *Star Wars*. I love having a little brother that's always in my corner.

To my cousin Ryan: You are a natural born caregiver. Thank you for looking out for Grandma, her house, and her cats. I am so proud that you are working in education and coaching young women.

To my cousin Sophia: You remind me so much of myself, and you give me faith in queers of the next generation. Keep creating your own path and being the badass Dom Bitch you are!

Aunt Becca and Uncle Otto, you have been a third set of parents for me and have worked tirelessly to keep our family together and our culture alive through countless dinners and seders. I appreciate all the care, support, and kindness you bring to our family, and all you have done to help me on my journey.

Tera: While we got off to a very rough start, I have enjoyed getting to know you in my adult life. Thank you so much for sharing your story last summer and for loving me like a son. I'm happy to have you in my life and to call you mom.

Matt: My mom has thrived with you, and I couldn't be happier to have you in my life. Thank you for opening you home to me and Daenerys. I'm sorry for never remembering how to turn off your TV.

Warren: We've grown apart over the years, but that doesn't mean I don't love you. Please keep loving Taylor and shield her from those who refuse to accept her.

Nonna: You once told me it's better if we're not friends on Facebook, and I respect that. With that being said, I hope you don't read this book. I love you and treasure slowly learning your fabulous recipes.

To David aka Rox aka Roxy-Cotton Candy: We have grown up together, lived together twice, and overcome so many obstacles. You are truly like a brother to me. I am excited to watch you succeed with Militia in LA, and I love every time we get to reconnect and inspire each other.

Amp: I still have the leather notebook you gave me after I first told you that I wanted to write a book. Well, here it is! You and Kris are part of my chosen family, and you are one of my best friends. You inspire me to be creative. Whenever I think I cannot do something or that I'm not good enough, you get me out of my head.

Jake aka Dextra De Novo: I blame you — officially! — for my Drag Race addiction. It's the healthiest addiction I have. You were quiet in law school, and now you are a fierce queen. Thank you for teaching me how to write a Bar Exam essay. I was on the verge of giving up, and you lifted me. I'm beyond excited to grow Reading is Fundamental with you.

Jackie: You're the Nick to my Demi. You continue to inspire me. You live a life I want to live. I love watching you evolve more and more into the Power Gay I want to emulate.

Amy: You also are responsible for helping me pass the California State Bar. You've always had my back and helped me learn to write more professionally. I love you!

Turbo: I have cherished our work sessions and getting to know you better over the past year. Thanks for having me over almost every weekend and exchanging ideas with me. I don't think I could have finished this book without our regular meetings.

Race: You have always been a role model and mentor, both as a writer and in my development as a leatherman. I admire how incredibly open-minded and accepting you are of all walks of life. Thank you for sharing your insight and encouraging me to try out new things.

Peaches Christ: I joined your show coming off a major relapse and being in outpatient rehab. Performing in your haunted house gave me accountability and a reason to stay present in life. Thank you for being part of what saved me. I love that you get excited about all of the weird horror things that excite me, too.

Frank Strona: Your mentorship has been invaluable to me and has helped me figure out what kind of person and professional I want to be. Thank you for your guidance and for the countless hours you spent helping me to create a new vision for myself.

Jon Knott: Thank you for helping me start a new life on my own in San Francisco!

Sister Roma: You have always been kind and supportive of me. Years ago, I heard you speak at Castro Country Club's gala about your journey with sobriety. You said that sobriety means community — it's the connections you make — not just meetings and steps. You and Michael have always been an inspiration throughout my recovery.

Cynthia: You give the best pep talks! I think most of the professional confidence I've developed has come from our conversations. You've encouraged me to dream big and to aim high, and I am so grateful for the self-worth that you have inspired within me.

Morris Ratner: You are the mentor who told me that I would be happier in life if I didn't silo my past and my sexuality. You taught me not to hide. This was a groundbreaking concept for me and still shapes how I approach my career today. Thank you!

My Darling Daenerys: You're a dog and you can't read this. You'll never know how you saved my life. How you gave me a reason to come home at times when I wanted to disappear for days. How you comforted and snuggled with me when no one else would stick around. You are so loving, loyal, and sweet (to me).

And, finally, to my beloved Grandma: It took writing this book to realize that my meth use resurfaced the same year that you died. You were my favorite human being ever, and I think that when you died, a part of me just checked out. I had been living on autopilot for so long, trying to achieve as many goals as possible that I think will bring me happiness. I'm finally starting to feel like myself again, and I know you would be proud of me. I miss you.

About the Author

Stephan Ferris is an accomplished Queer legal scholar and activist attorney. His most recent work has been published in Harvard's *LGBTQ Policy Journal*. He is part of an emerging generation of openly Queer and sexually progressive activist attorneys who see the law as an opportunity to make social, civic, and cultural change. He advances his views and work to a wide range of audiences through published scholarly articles and speaking engagements related to sexual health, activism, and the law. He contributes his expertise to the Practising Law Institute and is a board director for Bay Area Lawyers for Individual Freedom. He lives in San Francisco's Castro District.

Image Credits

p. 22, Photo courtesy of the author.

p. 31, Photo courtesy of the author.

p. 37, Photo courtesy of the author.

p. 70, Photo courtesy of the author.

p. 116, Witness Statement courtesy of the author.

p. 135, Photo courtesy of the author.

p. 145, Photo courtesy of the author.

p. 175, Photo credit: Georg Lester.

p. 184, Photo credit: Inked Kenny.

About the Type and Paper

Designed by Malou Verlomme of the Monotype Studio, Macklin is an elegant, high-contrast typeface. It has been designed purposely for more emotional appeal.

The concept for Macklin began with research on historical material from Britain and Europe dating to the beginning of the 19th century, specifically the work of Vincent Figgins. Verlomme pays respect to Figgins's work with Macklin, but pushes the family to a more contemporary place.

This book is printed on natural Rolland Enviro Book stock. The paper is 100 percent post-consumer sustainable fiber content and is FSC-certified.

Unbound Edition Press champions honest, original voices. Committed to the power of writers who explore and illuminate the contemporary human condition, we publish collections of poetry, short fiction, and essays. Our publisher and editorial team aim to identify, develop, and defend authors who create thoughtfully challenging work which may not find a home with mainstream publishers. We are guided by a mission to respect and elevate emerging, under-appreciated, and marginalized authors, with a strong commitment to advancing LGBTQ+ and BIPOC voices. We are honored to make meaningful contributions to the literary arts by publishing their work.

unboundedition.com